AF608193

DEPRIVATION OF THE CLERICAL GARB

A Historical Synopsis and a Commentary

THE CATHOLIC UNIVERSITY OF AMERICA
CANON LAW STUDIES
No. 334

Deprivation of the Clerical Garb

A Historical Synopsis and a Commentary

A DISSERTATION

SUBMITTED TO THE FACULTY OF THE SCHOOL OF CANON LAW OF THE CATHOLIC UNIVERSITY OF AMERICA IN PARTIAL FULFILLMENT OF THE REQUIREMENTS FOR THE DEGREE OF DOCTOR OF CANON LAW

BY

REVEREND JOSEPH A. SHIELDS, A.B., J.C.L.
PRIEST OF THE ARCHDIOCESE OF PHILADELPHIA

THE CATHOLIC UNIVERSITY OF AMERICA PRESS
WASHINGTON, D. C.
1958

NIHIL OBSTAT:

EDUARDUS G. ROELKER, S.T.D., J.C.D.
Censor deputatus
Washingtonii, D. C., die 26 Augusti, 1957

IMPRIMATUR:

✠ IOANNES FRANCISCUS O'HARA, C.S.C., D.D.
Archiepiscopus Philadelphiensis
Philadelphiae, die 28 Augusti, 1957

MURRAY AND HEISTER, INC.
WASHINGTON, D. C.

PRINTED BY
TIMES AND NEWS PUBLISHING CO.
GETTYSBURG, PA., U. S. A.

To
His Excellency
The Most Reverend Jerome D. Hannan, S.T.D., J.C.D., LL.B.
Bishop of Scranton
in appreciation

TABLE OF CONTENTS

TABLE OF CONTENTS (Continued)

TABLE OF CONTENTS (Continued)

CHAPTER PAGE

PART TWO

Canonical Commentary

TABLE OF CONTENTS (Continued)

FOREWORD

For a proper understanding of any of the vindicative penalties peculiar to clerics listed in canon 2298 of the Code of Canon Law, a familiarity with pre-Code canonical legislation pertinent to that penalty is of the greatest value. To provide such a historical background for one of the gravest of these penalties, viz., deprivation of the clerical garb, is the purpose of the first part of this dissertation. Since this penalty, however, was not constituted as a separate and distinct punishment in the penal legislation of the Church until the binding enactment of the Code in 1918, the writer has found it necessary to present the historical antecedents of this penalty in a rather indirect fashion. Rather than forego entirely the benefits to be derived from such a historical study, he has deemed it wise to present a brief history of the penalties which in the years prior to 1918 served as punishment for clerics who were scandalous and incorrigible in their conduct, and which at the same time effected a loss of the clerical privileges and of the charitable sustenance now made mandatory for deposed clerics in canon 2303, § 2, of the Code. The history of these penalties has been chosen because scandal and incorrigibility are the very reasons why deprivation of the clerical garb is inflicted today, and because these effects are the very ones now ascribed to the latter penalty. By analogy, then, if deprivation of the clerical garb ever existed as part of a more generic penalty, it would have been in penalties inflicted for such reasons and causing such effects, as the following pages of introduction to the historical synopsis will demonstrate.

In the second part of the dissertation the writer has attempted to supply in some small measure for the almost complete lack of canonical commentary relative to deprivation of the clerical garb. Most of the general commentators on the laws of the Code (and even those who profess as their specialized aim the presentation of a commentary on the Church's penal law) have contented themselves with setting down what amounts to nothing more than a translation of the Latin text of canons 2300 and 2304 into the various vernacular tongues in which they wrote. Even those authors who have written their commentaries in Latin have for the most part merely paraphrased the pertinent canons rather than presented a commentary on them. One should not be surprised at such a dearth of commentary in view of the comparative newness of the penalty in question. To compensate for this woeful lack of detail, the writer has made an attempt herein to present a canonical commentary on this penalty alone. Of necessity the commentary of reputable authors relative to kindred penalties (notably deposition and degradation) will have to be taken into consideration. In this latter portion of the dissertation, therefore, the writer will strive to clarify deprivation of the garb with all the pertinent data which authors present when commenting on most other canonical penalties. Accordingly, he will make an investigation into the nature of the penalty, the effects which are necessarily consequent upon it, the proper active and passive subject for its infliction, the method in which it is to be inflicted, and, finally, the way in which it ceases.

A few words are called for concerning the choice of the spelling "vindicative" rather than the more common "vindictive." While it is true that the spelling "vindictive" has the meaning of "punitive," and so may well convey the *purpose* of the Church in inflicting this penalty as expressed in canon 2286, it is equally true that this spelling in its first meaning, as any dictionary will confirm, connotes the idea of revenge and hate, ideas which are manifestly alien to the *spirit* in which the Church inflicts this penalty.[1] In inflicting this penalty, the Church intends not so much to punish the individual as to restore the social order, render justice triumphant, and rehabilitate public faith and tranquillity, all of which are contained in the concept of *vindication.*[2]

The writer wishes to avail himself of this opportunity to express

---

[1] Canon 2214, § 2; cf. Cloran, *Previews and Practical Cases, Code of Canon Law, Book V, Delicts and Penalties* (Milwaukee: Bruce Publishing Co., 1951), p. 202 (hereafter cited as *Previews and Practical Cases*); Christ, *Dispensation From Vindicative Penalties,* Catholic University of America Canon Law Studies, n. 174 (Washington, D. C.: Catholic University of America Press, 1943), pp. xii-xiii.

[2] Cf. Ottaviani, *Institutiones Iuris Publici Ecclesiastici* (2. ed., 2 vols., Typis Polyglottis Vaticanis, 1936), I, 132-133.

his heartfelt gratitude towards His Excellency, the Most Reverend John F. O'Hara, C.S.C., D.D., for the opportunity of completing the graduate course in canon law at The Catholic University of America, which course had been undertaken by the writer through the goodness of his predecessor as Archbishop of Philadelphia, His Eminence, the late Dennis Cardinal Dougherty; towards the Faculty of the School of Canon Law, for their kind direction and valuable assistance; and to all others who have helped in any way in the completion of this work.

PART ONE

Historical Synopsis

INTRODUCTION

Law as a ruling force in the government of any human society can be considered under two very different aspects. If one chooses to take into consideration only the stable substratum of the law, which remains essentially the same over a period of years regardless of accidental changes, then law can be looked upon as something static. It is in this sense that authors speak of law as being perpetual.[1] Or, quite the opposite, one can view law as a really dynamic entity, constantly changing as the lawmaker perceives the need of change to meet the demands of new times and new circumstances. This change may come about in several ways: by complete revocation of the former law, by its partial abolition, by supplementary additions to the law, and so forth.[2]

One must be careful, however, to distinguish from mere change that which one might term a certain evolution of the law, whereby the lawmaker only makes more explicit in the new law what was already implicit in the old, or, if one prefers, constitutes as new law the several specific component parts of a hitherto single generic law. Canon law is no exception to the truth of these general principles. Their verity is especially evident in the historical conspectus of the vindicative penalty peculiar to clerics, which this dissertation strives to present, viz., the evolution of ecclesiastical legislation depriving clerics of their right to wear the clerical garb.

For centuries deprivation of the clerical garb *qua talis* was

---

[1] For a more thorough treatment of this viewpoint, cf. Michiels, *Normae Generales Iuris Canonici* (2. ed., 2 vols., Paris: Desclée et Socii, 1949), I, 176 (hereafter cited as *Normae Generales*); Van Hove, *Commentarium Lovaniense in Codicem Iuris Canonici*, Vol. I, tom. II, *De Legibus Ecclesiasticis* (Mechliniae-Romae: H. Dessain, 1930), nn. 87-90 (hereafter cited as *De Legibus Ecclesiasticis*).

[2] Cf. c. 24, *de sententia excommunicationis*, V, 11, in VI°, where in the words of Pope Boniface VIII, "Alma Mater Ecclesia plerumque nonnulla rationabiliter ordinat et consulte, quae suadente subiectorum utilitate postmodum consultius ac rationabilius revocat in meliusve commutat."

nowhere inflicted as a specific penalty in itself. As such it is a new penalty and dates only from the time of the enactment of the Code of Canon Law.[3] Rather was it looked upon as a concomitant part of the more generic vindicative penalties of deposition and degradation. These two formed the stable substratum which down through the years produced the peculiar effects now ascribed to deprivation of the clerical garb. Even today one sees *perpetual* deprivation of the clerical garb referred to among authors of commentaries and writers of dissertations as "aggravated deposition" and "mitigated degradation."[4]

Hence, if one is to shed any light on the history of the penalty which this dissertation treats of *ex professo,* it is to the history of deposition and degradation that one must turn. Rendering the history of this penalty even more obscure and enigmatic is the fact that even deposition and degradation themselves were not looked upon as two separate and distinct penalties until the Church, whose penal code was to embrace them as integral parts of its penitential discipline, had passed through twelve turbulent centuries in its history.[5]

---

[3] Cf. Wernz-Vidal, *Ius Canonicum ad Codicis Normam Exactum* (7 toms. in 8 vols., Romae: apud Aedes Universitatis Gregorianae, 1923-1938), VII (1937), p. 367, n. 349, V, and p. 377, n. 352 (hereafter cited as *Ius Canonicum*). The complete lack of any footnotes in the Code itself with reference to canon 2298, 9°, 11°, also argues for the newness of this penalty as a distinct penalty.

[4] Cf., e.g., Ayrinhac-Lydon, *Penal Legislation in the New Code of Canon Law* (New York: Benziger Bros., 1936), p. 126, n. 166 (hereafter cited as *Penal Legislation*); Findlay, *Canonical Norms Governing the Deposition and Degradation of Clerics,* Catholic University of America Canon Law studies, n. 130 (Washington, D. C.: Catholic University of America Press, 1941), pp. 172, 206 (hereafter cited as *Deposition and Degradation*).

[5] Cf. Du Cange, *Glossarium ad Scriptores Mediae et Infimae Latinitatis* (ed. nova, Parisiis, 1937-1938), s.v., "Degradatio" (hereafter cited as *Glossarium . . . Latinitatis*); Kober, *Die Deposition und Degradation nach den Grundsätzen des kirchlichen Rechts, historisch-dogmatisch dargestellt* (Tübingen, 1867), p. 130 (hereafter cited as *Die Deposition und Degradation*); Chelodi, *Ius Poenale et Ordo Procedendi in Iudiciis Criminalibus iuxta Codicem Iuris Canonici* (Tridenti, 1925 [1920?]), p. 66 (hereafter cited as *Ius Poenale*); Devoti, *Institutionum Canonicarum Libri IV* (ed. prima Romana post quintam, Romae, 1825), § XIX, n. 2, p. 389 (hereafter

Obviously, such a history, gleaned as it is from the combined history of what now constitute two other distinct penalties in the penal legislation of the Code, will leave something to be desired. To a large degree it is bound to be a matter of deduction and conjecture. If, however, one keeps in mind that even today deprivation of the clerical garb though distinct from,[6] is still closely akin to,[7] degradation and deposition, one will realize that such conclusions and hypotheses will not fall too far short of the truth. Let it be understood from the outset, however, that this dissertation does not intend, nor indeed pretend, to narrate an exhaustive history of deposition and degradation in themselves. The history of those two penalties has already been presented at some length in an earlier dissertation of The Catholic University of America Canon Law Studies.[8] Rather will the writer be content to offer a presentation of the history of deposition and degradation only in so far as these two penalties were inflicted for the reasons which now demand the deprivation of the clerical garb as their punishment, or in so far as their infliction brought about effects now attributed to deprivation of the clerical garb.

Wherefore, in the following pages of the historical commentary, whenever deposition or degradation is mentioned as being inflicted because of scandal on the part of any given cleric coupled with his refusal to amend even after repeated warnings, such an infliction will, in the light of the present legislation, be presumed

cited as *Institutiones*); Lega, *Praelectiones in Textum Iuris Canonici De Delictis et Poenis* (2. ed., Romae, 1910), p. 281 (hereafter cited as *De Delictis et Poenis*); Wernz, *Ius Decretalium* (1. ed., 6 vols., Prati et Romae, 1898-1913), VI, 121, n. 119; Benedictus Pp. XIV, *De synodo dioecesana* (2. ed., 2 vols., Parmae, 1764), lib. IX, cap. 6, n. 3.

[6] Cf. canon 2298, 9°, 10°, 11°, 12°, where temporal deprivation of the clerical garb, deposition, perpetual deprivation of the clerical garb, and degradation are enumerated as four distinct vindicative penalties peculiar to clerics.

[7] Cf. canon 2304, § 1, which demands previous deposition as one of the prerequisites for perpetual deprivation of the clerical garb, and canon 2305, § 1, which lists perpetual deprivation of the clerical garb along with deposition and reduction to the lay state as the three constituent elements of degradation.

[8] Findlay, *Deposition and Degradation*. It is n. 130 in that series.

to have included a penal deprivation of the clerical garb.[9] In a similar fashion, whenever either of these penalties is mentioned as having resulted in a prohibition to exercise any ecclesiastical functions, or in a deprivation of the clerical privileges, or as having freed the ordinary from any obligation in charity of providing for the support of a deposed cleric, such an effect will, again on an analogy to modern ecclesiastical legislation, be presumed to have resulted from an implicit deprivation of the clerical garb.[10]

In the attempt to present a resumé of the penalty's history, it will be necessary to test the validity of these presumptions. This the writer hopes to accomplish by discussing briefly just what is meant by the clerical garb, habit, or dress, which is the object of the deprivation that this penalty inflicts, and then by investigating whether or not such a distinctive garb existed from the very beginning of the Church's history. Obviously, if no such special garb existed at any specified time in the Church's history, the penalties of deposition and degradation, even though inflicted at that time for reasons similar to the reasons given by the Code for deprivation of the clerical garb today, or even though they resulted then in effects ascribed to deprivation of the clerical garb by modern legislation, could hardly have contained even an implicit deprivation of the clerical garb at that particular time. Rather would they be considered then as forerunners or precedents of the penalty in question.

---

[9] Cf. canons 2300 and 2304, § 1, where the giving of scandal (*si clericus gravia scandala praebeat; si clericus depositus . . . scandalum dare pergat*) and incorrigibility (*si clericus . . . monitus non resipiscat*) are given as the reasons for inflicting deprivation of the clerical garb.

[10] Cf. canons 2300 and 2304, § 2, where these effects are listed as consequent on the deprivation of the clerical garb.

CHAPTER I

THE CLERICAL GARB, HABIT, OR DRESS, WHICH IS THE OBJECT OF THIS PENALTY, AND ITS EVOLUTION

ARTICLE 1. MEANING OF THE TERM, "CLERICAL GARB"

In discussing the penalty of temporary deprivation of the clerical garb, Augustine (1872-1943) made the statement that this penalty "refers, of course, to the usual clerical garb and tonsure, not the vestments used in the sacred ministry."[1] Since this dissertation, as has already been noted, intends to treat the history of deprivation of the clerical garb as implicit in the history of deposition and degradation, a difficulty immediately presents itself, viz., the stripping of vestments concomitant with the infliction of deposition and degradation would seem to be a removal of the vestments used in the sacred ministry rather than a deprivation of the cleric's ordinary dress.[2] Yet these sacred vestments are precisely the ones which Augustine maintains are not referred to in deprivation of the clerical garb. How then can a penal deprivation of the clerical garb (the term being understood as Augustine understands it) be proved from the history of deposition and degradation? The following observations may help to elucidate the matter.

ARTICLE 2. INTRODUCTION OF A SPECIAL GARB FOR USE AT SACRED FUNCTIONS

First of all, there is no clear-cut evidence for the first three centuries of the Church's existence that clerics used any special

[1] (Bachofen), Charles Augustine, *A Commentary on the New Code of Canon Law* (8 vols., St Louis: Herder & Co., Vol. VIII, 3. ed., 1931), VIII, 259 (hereafter cited as *Commentary*).

[2] Cf. *The Catholic Encyclopedia* (15 vols., index and 2 suppls., New York, 1907-1922), IV, 738, s.v., "deposition," where it is stated that deposition was almost always coupled with the ceremony of divesting delinquents of the garments used in the function of their *sacred ministry;* c. 2, *de poenis,* V, 9, in VI°, where Boniface VIII (1294-1303), in reply to the Bishop of Béziers, gave a detailed account of the method to be observed in the removing of the *sacred* vestments from a degraded cleric.

dress when engaged in divine services.[3] About the beginning of the fourth century, however, with the end of the era of persecution and the advent of the Emperor Constantine (306-337), a distinction began to be made between the everyday wear of the clergy and the vestments used by them in sacred functions. Constantine himself is said to have presented Macarius, Bishop of Jerusalem, with a rich vestment, embroidered in gold, to be used by him in the ceremony of baptizing.[4] Not long afterwards, St. Athanasius (295-373) was condemned by his adversaries for imposing a tax upon the Egyptians in order to provide a fund for the purchasing of linen vestments to be used in the Church.[5] Such vestments must have been in use at the time, otherwise there would have been no need of setting up a fund to provide for them. St. Jerome (ca. 342-420) also distinguished between a secular and a sacred garment when, in his Dialogue against the Pelagians, he asked what hostility would be manifested towards God, if he should use a cleaner garment, or if any other member of the clerical order should come forth in a white vestment when he administered the sacraments.[6] Other references to special garments for the sacred functions were made by St. John Chrysostom (ca. 345-407) in reference to the sacred vestments

---

[3] Cf. Bingham, *The Antiquities of the Christian Church* (reprinted from original edition, 2 vols., London, 1856), I, 645 (hereafter cited as *Antiquities*); McCloud, *Clerical Dress and Insignia of the Roman Catholic Church* (Milwaukee: Bruce, 1948), p. vii (in foreword of Rev. William J. Lallou, S.T.D.). This work will hereafter be cited as *Clerical Dress and Insignia.*

[4] Cf. Bingham, *loc. cit.;* McCloud, *loc. cit.*

[5] *Apologia contra Arianos,*—Migne, *Patrologiae Cursus Completus, Series Graeca* (161 vols., Parisiis, 1857-1866), XXV, 358 (hereafter cited as *MPG*); Sozomenus, *Historia Ecclesiastica,* II, 22—*MPG,* LXVII, 991, and Schaff and Wace, *Nicene and Post-Nicene Fathers of the Christian Church* (Second Series, 2 vols., New York, 1890), II, 272 (hereafter cited as Schaff).

[6] *Dialogus adversus Pelagianos,* lib. I—Migne, *Patrologiae Cursus Completus, Series Latina* (221 vols., Parisiis, 1844-1855), XXIII, 524 (hereafter cited as *MPL*); cf. also Jerome's letter to Heliodorus, wherein he states that Nepotian used the *pallium,* a cloak that was in ordinary use among Christian philosophers, for ordinary wear, but a tunic for his sacred functions; *Ep. LX,—MPL,* XXII, 597.

of deacons;[7] by Sozomenus (fl. early 5th century), when speaking of priests and deacons being beaten and driven out of the church, clad as they were in the vestments of their ministrations;[8] and by St. Gregory Nazianzen (329-389), in adverting to the deacon's dress.[9]

Councils of the same and the succeeding periods which referred to a special clerical garb for use in the sacred functions are the Council of Laodicea (343/381) concerning the *orarion*, the primitive stole;[10] the reputed IV Council of Carthage (398) speaking of the *alba*;[11] the Council of Narbonne (589) in southern France, also in reference to the *alba*;[12] the I (II) Council of Braga (561 or 563) in Spain, with reference to the *orarion* again;[13] the III (IV) Council of Braga (675), speaking of the *orarion*;[14] and the IV Council of Toledo (633) in Spain, with reference to the *orarion* of deacons, and the vestments to be restored to clerics who had been unjustly deposed.[15]

---

[7] *In Matthaeum Hom. LXXXII al. LXXXIII,—MPG,* LVIII, 745.

[8] *Historia Ecclesiastica,* VIII, 21,—*MPG,* LXVII, 1570; Schaff, II, 412.

[9] *Somnium de Anastasiae Ecclesia, quam in urbe Constantini exstruxit—MPG,* XXXVII, 1253.

[10] Canons 22 and 23—Bruns, *Canones Apostolorum et Conciliorum Saeculorum IV, V, VI, VII* (2 vols., Berlin, 1839), I, 76 (hereafter cited as Bruns).

[11] Canon 41—Bruns, I, 145; Hardouin, *Acta Conciliorum et Epistolae Decretales ac Constitutiones Summorum Pontificum* (12 vols., Parisiis, 1714-1715), L, 981 (hereafter cited as Hardouin); Mansi, *Sacrorum Conciliorum Nova et Amplissima Collectio* (53 vols. in 59, Parisiis-Arnhem-Leipzig, 1901-1927), III, 954 (hereafter cited as Mansi). This legislation is incorrectly attributed to a IV Council of Carthage. Actually it is part of a collection known as the *Statuta Ecclesiae Antiqua,* which originated in the city of Arles shortly before the time of St. Caesarius of Arles' episcopate (503-543). The collection is composed of canons of Greek councils and decretals of Roman Pontiffs. Cf. Van Hove, *Commentarium Lovaniense in Codicem Iuris Canonici,* Vol. I, tomus I, *Prolegomena ad Codicem Iuris Canonici* (Mechliniae-Romae: H. Dessain, 1928), Vol. I, tom. I, n. 149 (hereafter cited as *Prolegomena*).

[12] Canon 12—Bruns, II, 61; Hardouin, III, 493; Mansi, IX, 1017.

[13] Canon 9—Bruns, II, 34; Hardouin, III, 351; Mansi, IX, 778.

[14] Canon 3 (4)—Bruns, II, 99; Hardouin, III, 1034; Mansi, XI, 156.

[15] Canon 40—Bruns, I, 234; Hardouin, III, 588; Mansi, X, 629; canon 28—Bruns, I, 231; Hardouin, III, 586; Mansi, X, 627.

ARTICLE 3. INTRODUCTION OF A SPECIAL GARB FOR CLERIC'S ORDINARY WEAR

It seems that a special garb as used *outside* the sanctuary did not exist much before the sixth century.[16] Augustine stated that the garb worn by clerics was nothing else originally than the old Roman dress, i.e., a tunic without sleeves (*collobium*) and a long white coat with sleeves (*dalmatica* or *tunica manicata et talaris*).[17] Bingham (1668-1723) foreshadowed Augustine in this view concerning the garb of the ancient clergy, when he stated that "such a decent mean was to be observed, as might keep them from obloquy and censure on both hands, either as too nice and critical, or too slovenly and careless in their dress: their habit being generally to be such, as might express the gravity of their minds without any superstitious singularities, and their modesty and humility without affectation. In this matter, therefore, their rules were formed according to the customs and opinions of the age, which are commonly the standard and measure of decency and indecency in things of this nature."[18] He then added that for several centuries there was no other evident distinction observed between the ordinary apparel of the cleric and the layman save the distinction inherent in the fact that the former was more constrained to wear that which was modest and grave, and becoming his state in life, without being compelled to wear any

---

[16] Augustine, *Commentary,* II (6. ed., 1936), 84; Bingham, *Antiquities,* I, 231; McCloud, *Clerical Dress and Insignia,* pp. vii, 37. Cf., however, Ferraris, *Prompta Bibliotheca, Canonica, Iuridica, Moralis, Theologica, necnon Ascetica, Polemica, Rubricistica, Historica* (9 vols., Romae, 1885-1899), Vol. II (1886), p. 305, s.v., "clericus," art. I, *Quoad ea quae concernunt Clerici nomen, habitum, et tonsuram,* nn. 76-78, where it is said that clerics wore no distinct garb for everyday wear before the *fifth* century, and the editor takes the opportunity to state that in his opinion this distinction was made even prior to that time. He offers no convincing arguments for his opinion, however, and the present writer will adhere to the opinion first cited as safer in practice. Hereafter Ferraris' work will be cited as *Prompta Bibliotheca.*

[17] Cf. *Commentary, loc. cit.;* cf. also Bingham, *op. cit.,* I, 232; McCloud, *op. cit.,* pp. viii and 37.

[18] Cf. *Antiquities,* I, 228.

determined garb or form of clothing.[19] In the course of time several councils and synods legislated on the subject, but they did not specify what kind of clothing was to be worn other than that it should not border on luxury or any affected neatness, but rather should manifest a happy medium between finery and slovenliness.[20]

According to Bingham, it seems that the use of a specific garb in daily wear by the clergy came about in the late fifth or early sixth century as a result of the fact that the clergy gradually came to be composed chiefly of philosophers and ascetics, men who all along had worn a distinctive garb, the *pallium* or cloak, as evidence that they were such.[21] Prior to that time it happened that various members of the clergy tried without success to introduce the *pallium* as a specific garb for members of the clerical order. In Asia Minor, the Council of Gangra (340/341) condemned Eustathius of Sebaste (ca. 300-ca. 377) for attempting to introduce the *pallium* of the ascetics in place of the *birrus* (the common tunic worn by members of the secular clergy and indeed by Christians generally). "If any man uses the *pallium* or cloak, upon the account of an ascetic life, and, as if there were some holiness in that, condemns those who with reverence use the *birrus,* and other garments that are commonly worn, let him be

---

[19] Bingham, *op. cit.,* I, 229-230.

[20] Cf., e.g., canon 45 of the *Statuta Ecclesiae Antiqua*—Bruns, I, 146; Hardouin, I, 982; Mansi, III, 955; canon 20 of the Council of Agde (506)—Bruns, II, 150; Hardouin, II, 1000; Mansi, VIII, 328. For other examples of similar legislation in later centuries, cf. McCloud, *Clerical Dress and Insignia,* pp. 37-39.

[21] Cf. *Antiquities,* I, 231; Ferraris, *Prompta Bibliotheca,* II, 306, s.v., "clericus," art. I, n. 83. Because of the dearth of primary sources on the subject, it must remain rather doubtful whether or not the clergy was composed chiefly of ascetics and philosophers at that time, and whether or not the *pallium* which they wore, according to Bingham, was the origin of a specific daily garb for clerics. Indeed the editor of *Prompta Bibliotheca,* in a footnote, expresses his displeasure with the opinion, though he does not offer any other opinion. At any rate, the *pallium* here in question would not have been the *pallium* as commonly understood now, a symbol of the archiepiscopal authority, but rather some sort of garment or scarf. Cf. Eidenschink, *The Election of Bishops in the Letters of Gregory the Great,* Catholic University of America Canon Law Studies, n. 215 (Washington, D. C.: Catholic University of America Press, 1945), pp. 101, 137.

anathema."[22] Sozomenus related that Eustathius himself, after this condemnation by the synod, reverted to the ordinary garb that the secular priests wore.[23] In the churches of Gaul, years later, the clergy still used the same secular garb as other Christians, and when some attempted to substitute the ascetical or philosophical cloak for it, Pope Celestine (422-432) reprimanded them. He demanded to know why that habit, the cloak, was used in the churches of Gaul, when it had been the custom of so many bishops for so many years to use the common habit of the people, from whom the clergy were to be distinguished by their doctrine, and not by their garb; by their conversation, not by their habit; by the purity of their souls, rather than by their dress.[24]

By way of exception, however, some ascetics in particular places were permitted to retain the *pallium* even after becoming clerics. Thus the priest Nepotian (+395/396) wore his *pallium* to the day of his death, even after his ordination to the priesthood.[25] Eusebius of Caesarea (263-339) related the same of Heraclas (180-247/248), who donned the philosopher's garb when he entered the neo-Platonic school of philosophy conducted by Ammonius (175-242), and continued to wear it even as a priest in Alexandria.[26]

ARTICLE 4. COLOR OF THE GARB

Even as to the color of the garb, centuries were to pass before any definite regulations were laid down concerning it. St. Jerome advised Nepotian that he should wear neither black nor white clothing, for gaiety and slovenliness were both equally reprehensible, the one savoring of nicety and delicacy, the other of vain glory.[27] Yet different customs prevailed in different locales. At Constantinople, in the time of the intruder Arsacius (+405)

---

[22] Canon 12—Bruns, I, 108; Hardouin, I, 535; Mansi, II, 1102 (Gentianus Hervetus), 1107 (Dionysius Exiguus), 1111 (Isidorus Mercator), 1114 (e Codice Lucensi). Translation in Bingham, *Antiquities, loc. cit.*

[23] *Historia Ecclesiastica,* III, 14—*MPG,* LXVII, 1079; Schaff, II, 294.

[24] *Ep. II ad Episc. Gall.,* c. 1—Hardouin, I, 1258; Mansi, IV, 465.

[25] St. Jerome (*Epitaphium Nepotiani, Ep. LX*)—*MPL,* XXII, 597.

[26] *Historia Ecclesiastica* (quoting Origen), VI, 19—*MPG,* XX, 570.

[27] *Ep. LII* (*Ep. II ad Nepotianum*)—MPL, XXII, 535.

and of St. John Chrysostom (+407), clerics commonly wore black to distinguish themselves from the Novatians, who wore white. This is apparent from a dispute between Sisinnius, a Novatian bishop, and one of Arsacius' clergy, which is related by Socrates (ca. 380-ca. 450).[28]

Lydon says that black as the color of suits, hats, etc., has been prescribed by force of law everywhere since the fifteenth century, in which matter the individual bishops cannot dispense, but need a special indult, e.g., for certain missionary countries, where the wearing of white clothing is the custom.[29] This statement notwithstanding, the color of the clerical clothing may not have been determined even that late in the history of the Church, for in the sixteenth century the Council of Trent (1545-1563) merely required that "clerics always wear a dress conformable to their order, that by the propriety of their outward apparel they may show forth the inward uprightness of their morals."[30] Nothing was mentioned as to any specific color. Accordingly, McCloud seems more correct in his statement that black has been the color of the cleric's garb only since the seventeenth century.[31] Pope Sixtus V (1585-1590) called the dress demanded by the Council of Trent the *vestis talaris* or the cassock.[32]

ARTICLE 5. MEANING OF THE TERM, "CLERICAL GARB," IN THE UNITED STATES

In accordance with the interpretation which Pope Sixtus V had placed on the legislation of the Council of Trent, it seems that

---

[28] *Historia Ecclesiastica,* VI, 22—*MPG,* LXVII, 727; Schaff, II, 152.

[29] Cf. Lydon, *Ready Answers in Canon Law* (3. ed., New York: Benziger Bros., 1948), pp. 228-229.

[30] Sess. XIV, *de ref.,* c. 6; translation in Schroeder, *Canons and Decrees of the Council of Trent* (St. Louis: Herder, 1941), p. 110.

[31] Cf. *Clerical Dress and Insignia,* p. 45. McCloud bases his statement on a decree of Pope Urban VIII, issued on Nov. 26, 1624. The present writer was unable to locate such a decree in any of the collections available to him.

[32] Const. *Cum sacrosanctum,* 9 ian. 1589, § 2—*Codicis Iuris Canonici Fontes cura Emi Petri Card. Gasparri editi* (9 vols., Romae [postea Civitate Vaticana]: Typis Polyglottis Vaticanis, 1923-1939. Vols. VII-IX, *ed. cura et studio Emi Iustiniani Card. Serédi*), n. 167 (hereafter cited as *Fontes*). Cf. also Benedictus XIV, const. *Ad militantis,* 30 mart. 1742, § 26—*Fontes,* n. 326.

from that time onward clerics were obliged to wear at all times the cassock as their distinctive dress. By approved custom, however, the interpretation that what was prescribed by Pope Sixtus was the wearing of the cassock at least for sacred and public functions prevailed. Outside of such functions a shorter garb was allowed in accordance with the local customs of the various regions.[33]

Here in the United States, the long-standing legitimate custom grew into the estate of positive law through the enactment in which the III Plenary Council of Baltimore (1884) decreed that clerics were to wear the Roman collar and cassock at home and in the church, while outside the house they were, along with the wearing of the Roman collar, to wear a coat of black or somber color, the length of which reached to the knees. To this decree religious (inasmuch as they did not customarily wear the distinctive habit of their community outside their houses), as well as secular clerics, were expected to conform.[34] This prescription of the III Plenary Council has never been revoked. The Code itself, in its legislation on the matter, merely states that all clerics must wear an appropriate ecclesiastical garb which is in accord with the legitimate customs of the region and the prescriptions of the local ordinary. Furthermore, they need not wear the clerical tonsure in those countries where custom directs otherwise.[35]

According to Augustine, the obligation imposed by the III Plenary Council of wearing a coat extending to the knees is still binding; Barrett, however, thinks otherwise.[36] From the very beginning, as Barrett points out, this prescription was interpreted in a broad fashion to mean that clerics should conform more or less to the style adopted by conservative laymen. On the basis of this interpretation, there now exists a custom contrary to the

---

[33] Cf. Wernz, *Ius Decretalium,* II, n. 177.

[34] *Acta et Decreta Concilii Plenarii Baltimorensis Tertii* (Baltimorae: Typis Ioannis Murphy et Sociorum, 1886), n. 77.

[35] Canon 136, § 1.

[36] Cf. Augustine, *Commentary,* II, 84; Barrett, *A Comparative Study of the Councils of Baltimore and the Code of Canon Law,* Catholic University of America Canon Law Studies, n. 83 (Washington, D. C.: The Catholic University of America, 1932), pp. 48-49.

law. Indeed, the prescription of the III Plenary Council which is in question, itself modified an earlier law of the II Plenary Council (1866) whereby clerics were obliged to wear a coat which extended *below* the knees. It may readily be presumed, therefore, that the intention of the Fathers of the III Plenary Council was that clerics could adhere to the style adopted by conservative laymen.[37]

According to the opinion advanced by Barrett (which the present writer endorses as correct), the clerical garb which here in the United States can be made the object of the vindicative penalty in question consists of either the cassock and Roman collar (in the case of the secular clergy) or the religious habit (in the case of the clergy who are members of religious communities) and the black suit and Roman collar as well (in the case of either class of clerics). Clerics in minor orders are not obliged by the III Plenary Council of Baltimore to wear the Roman collar outside the house; they are to follow the custom of the region and the prescripts of their ordinary. In many places such clerics wear the ordinary collar with a black tie. Accordingly, in the event that the penalty in question needed to be inflicted, it is the deprivation of this garb that would be called for. As will be pointed out in a subsequent chapter of the canonical commentary, however, clerics in minor orders should not be made the subject of this penalty; rather, they should be reduced to the lay state immediately.

ARTICLE 6. CONCLUSIONS FROM THE PRECEDING ARTICLES

In the light of the preceding observations on the vicissitudes of the clerical garb itself during the course of the centuries, one can deduce the following logical conclusions concerning the history of the penalty whereby a delinquent cleric was deprived of that garb. First, since there is no certain evidence before the fourth century of any special clerical garb for use in the sacred functions and as distinct from that which the cleric ordinarily wore, it is most probable that the penalties of deposition and degradation in the Apostolic and the immediate post-Apostolic

[37] Cf. Barrett, *loc. cit.*

times did not even entail a deprivation of the sacred vestments worn by clerics. Secondly, since it is stated with good historic foundation that clerics did not differ from laymen in their ordinary garb before the late fifth or early sixth century, it is very likely that the penalties of deposition and degradation in the fourth and fifth centuries implied at most a deprivation of the sacred vestments alone. Thirdly, it is only from the end of the fifth or the beginning of the sixth century that deprivation of the cleric's ordinary garb could possibly have accompanied the infliction of the penalties of deposition and degradation. Hence it is only from the latter time onward that any apparent difficulty can arise in the attempt to trace the history of deprivation of the clerical garb (properly understood) as implicit in the history of deposition and degradation. From the sixth to the fourteenth century, therefore, one must be content with the deductions and conjectures mentioned in the introduction to this historical synopsis.

ARTICLE 7. EXPLICIT AND IMPLICIT LEGISLATION INVOLVING DEPRIVATION OF THE CLERICAL GARB

The apparent difficulty mentioned at the end of the preceding article disappears in the fourteenth century, when the ceremony of depriving a deposed or a degraded cleric of his vestments included a removal not only of the sacred vestments, but also of the clerical garb (properly so called) and the tonsure. This is evidenced by the letter of Pope Boniface VIII to the Bishop of Béziers, as cited at the beginning of this chapter, for after describing the way in which the *sacred* vestments were to be removed, the Sovereign Pontiff concluded with the admonition that there be removed from the delinquent cleric's head every trace of his clerical tonsure, and that there be taken from him also his clerical garb.[38] Even before the time of Boniface, however, one finds examples in history of a certain ceremonial accompanying the infliction of deposition. These examples serve to fortify the deductions and hypotheses which one is forced to make in those earlier periods. Moreover, men well versed in liturgy, while they freely admit that the earliest pontificals do not contain

[38] C. 2, *de poenis,* V, 9, in VI°.

any record of the way in which deposition was solemnly carried out, still are convinced that some ceremony was attached to the execution of this penalty.[39] Even as early as the fourth century, when clerics as yet wore no special garb in everyday life and had just begun to employ special vestments for the sacred ministry, Socrates related the case of Patriarch Eustathius' deposition by the Council of Antioch (330), and stated that all the bishops present reviled Eustathius, calling him "unholy." Evidently, there was some kind of ceremony being carried out.[40]

Baronius (1538-1607) related the story of a certain Irenaeus (+ ca. 450), who was expelled from the church of Tyre and suffered the loss of all his clerical insignia because of his adherence to the Nestorian heresy.[41] Since these two penalties were inflicted midway in the fourth and fifth centuries respectively, there probably was involved no deprivation of the clerical garb as such, but at least the ceremony attached to their infliction could be used as a precedent for such action when the clergy finally did begin to wear a distinctive garb shortly thereafter.

In the seventh century, one finds the IV Council of Toledo (633) decreeing that a formal procedure be observed in the restoration of an unjustly deposed cleric when he had been found innocent. The cleric's lost rank was to be given back before the altar, through a new bestowal of the stole, the ring, and the crozier, when a bishop has been thus victimized; through a new conferring of the stole and chasuble, in the case of a priest; through a new clothing with the stole and alb, when the case of a deacon was in question; and so forth, down through the inferior orders.[42] Since these vestments were to be restored to the wrongly

---

[39] Cf. Martène, *De Antiquis Ecclesiae Ritibus* (3 vols., Rotomagi, 1700-1702), III, c. 2, n. 1, Catalanus, *Pontificale Romanum* (3 vols., Parisiis, 1852), III, tit. VII, § 1; Maskell, *Monumenta Ritualia Ecclesiae Anglicanae* (3 vols., London, 1846-1847), III, p. cliii.

[40] *Historia Ecclesiastica,* I, 24—*MPG,* LXVII, 143.

[41] *Annales Ecclesiastici* (37 vols., Barri-Ducis, 1864-1883), VII (an. 448), n. 6.

[42] Canon 28—Bruns, I, 231; Hardouin, III, 586; Mansi, X, 627; cf. also Hinschius, *Das Kirchenrecht der Katholiken und Protestanten in Deutschland* (6 vols., Berlin, 1869-1897. Vols. I-IV, *System des katholischen Kirchenrechts,* Berlin, 1869-1888), IV, 809 (hereafter cited as *Kirchenrecht*).

punished cleric, it is not difficult to deduce the fact that there must have been a prior removal of the same vestments at the time of the unjust infliction of the penalty. Indeed, the same canon explicitly stated that (at least in the territory governed by the enactments of this council) the cleric could not be what he had formerly been, unless he received from the hand of the bishop before the altar the insignia which he had lost.[43] At first glance, one could be led to believe that the ceremony here described was one of reordination, and not merely a restoration of the sacred vestments unjustly taken from the cleric. Since the Council of Toledo was only a particular council, it is possible that it could have made such an error. There are a few cases of such prescribed reordinations in this period of church history, e.g., under order of John Scholasticus, Patriarch of Constantinople (564-578), of Pope Sergius III (904-911), and of Pope St. Leo IX (1049-1054).[44] Hefele (1809-1893), however, was of the opinion that a reordination was not undertaken in this instance, but that simply a restoration of the vestments was intended.[45]

In the ninth century, Ignatius, Patriarch of Constantinople (+877), was unjustly subjected to deposition. Baronius related that the Patriarch was stripped of his usual vestments, clad instead in tattered and dirty pontificals, which then were torn from him.[46] At the II General Council of the Lateran (1139) Pope Innocent II (1130-1143) deposed the followers of the deceased anti-Pope, Peter Leoni (Anacletus II). Calling each by name, as the onlookers derided them, he took from them their croziers, pallia, and rings.[47]

From these few cited examples one can easily see that some sort of ceremony was observed when the penalty of deposition was inflicted. Though for the most part there was no mention that

---

[43] Bruns, I, 231; Hardouin, III, 586; Mansi, X, 627; c. 65, C. XI, q. 3.

[44] Cf. Many, *Praelectiones de sacra ordinatione* (Parisiis, 1905), nn. 18-25, pp. 57-76.

[45] Cf. Hefele, *A History of the Christian Councils,* translated from the German and edited by William Clark (2. ed., 5 vols., Edinburgh, 1883-1896), IV, 453.

[46] *Annales Ecclesiastici,* XIV (an. 861), n. 7.

[47] Hardouin, VI, 1214.

the cleric's ordinary garb was taken away from him, still one can reasonably assume that this occurred along with the deprivation of his sacred vestments, which deprivation was explicitly mentioned, as is evident from the aforementioned quotations. Moreover, Pope Boniface, in his legislation on the matter, spoke of the removal of the cleric's ordinary garb and tonsure in such an offhand manner that one is forced to conclude that its deprivation, as well as the deprivation of the cleric's sacred vestments, was not an innovation made by Boniface, but rather a long-standing integral part of the ceremonial which always accompanied the infliction of the penalty of deposition. Hence, deprivation of the cleric's ordinary garb should probably be considered as implicit in the penalty of deposition from the sixth century onward. For the first five centuries, when no special garb was in use, deposition should probably be considered merely as one of the forerunners of the penalty at that time.

CHAPTER II

Pre-Code Antecedents of Deprivation of the Clerical Garb

Article 1. Forerunners of the Penalty in the First Five Centuries of the Christian Era

Since clerics did not wear any distinctive garb for ordinary wear until the early sixth century, all that one can hope to determine in the first five centuries of the Christian era is the penalty (or penalties) which served during this period as forerunners to deprivation of the clerical garb. Accordingly, one must look to see how the Church punished scandal and incorrigibility on the part of clerics at that time, and attempt to discover what penalty (or penalties) in the same era resulted in effects now attributed by the Code to deprivation of the clerical garb. In the following sections of this article it will be shown that deposition was the penalty usually then employed by the Church to punish such conduct and to cause such effects.

Section 1. Deposition as a Penalty for the Giving of Scandal and Incorrigibility

Before one commences to mention the various places in the legislation of antiquity where deposition is given as the penalty for crimes of clerics involving scandalous conduct and incorrigibility, one should duly recall the following two facts. First, over half of this period was passed in the age of the persecutions of the Church. Consequently one must not expect to find universal legislation regulating the various medicinal censures and vindicative penalties peculiar to clerics. Secondly, this age, as well as being the era of persecutions, was also the period of formation. Accordingly, one should not expect to encounter a unanimity of terminology even in regard to those penalties to whose existence historical records bear witness. It seems that St. Cyprian, bishop of Carthage (248-258), was the first to give a technical definition of the term, "deposition."[1] "Degradation," as technically understood, did not appear in canonical usage till half a century later at the Council of Elvira (ca. 306) in Spain.[2]

Even after their initial technical definition, however, the two terms continued to be used interchangeably in designation of one and the same penalty up until the beginning of the thirteenth century.[3] In this dissertation deposition will be the term employed up until the beginning of the thirteenth century, especially in view of the later distinct meaning given to degradation. Adding to the vagueness and ambiguity of the legal terminology of the period is the fact that other words and phrases were employed by different Pontiffs and divers councils in designation of the punishment denoted by the terms "deposition" and "degradation." This last statement is apparent from the following excerpts of early ecclesiastical legislation, which testify to the fact that deposition was inflicted in antiquity for the giving of scandal and for incorrigibility on the part of clerics.

Halfway through the third century, Rogatian, a bishop in Mauretania, wrote to St. Cyprian inquiring what was to be done with one of the deacons in his diocese who was guilty of disobedience and possessed of a rebellious attitude. Cyprian answered that Rogatian was entirely within his rights if he decided to depose him.[4] In 314, a council held at Arles, in Gaul, legislated that any cleric who was known *publicly* to have handed over the Sacred Scriptures, or the sacred vessels, or the names of fellow

---

[1] *Ep. LXV, III—MPL,* IV, 397; cf. *Corpus Scriptorum Ecclesiasticorum Latinorum* (70 vols., incomplete, Vindobonae: apud C. Geroldi Filium, Bibliopolam Academiae, 1866-), Vol. III, 3 parts, *S. Thasci Caecili Cypriani Opera Omnia* (recensuit et commentario critico instruxit Gulielmus Hartel, 1871), part 2, p. 472 (hereafter cited as *CSEL*); Kober, *Die Deposition und Degradation,* p. 5, n. 9; Aichner, *Compendium Iuris Ecclesiastici* (6. ed., Brixinae, 1887), § 220, p. 747, n. 8 (hereafter cited as *Compendium*).

[2] Canon 20—Hardouin, I, 252; c. 5, D. XLVII; Aichner, *Compendium, loc. cit.*

[3] Cf. Findlay, *Deposition and Degradation*, p. 6; cf. also fn. 5, p. xvi of this present dissertation.

[4] *Ep. LXV, III—MPL,* IV, 397; Mansi, I, 903; *CSEL,* Vol. III, part 2, p. 472.

Christians to the persecutors, was to be removed from the clerical order.[5] Particularly significant about this decree were the phrases that indicated what knowledge was requisite before action could be taken against the accused cleric. These phrases were "*ex actis publicis*" and "*non verbis nudis.*" In other words, this penalty of removal from the clerical order was inflicted on the guilty cleric not for the intrinsic malice alone of the crimes committed, but also because of the extrinsic element of scandal involved, since the commission of these crimes was of public knowledge.

The *Statuta Ecclesiae Antiqua* (wrongly attributed to the reputed IV Council of Carthage [398]) ruled, among other things, that a cleric who spoke evil, especially against priests, was to be degraded from office, if he was unwilling to seek pardon for his offense.[6] Here again one may note that the penalty of degradation was inflicted not solely for the sake of punishing the unadorned crime of speaking evil, but also because of some aggravating circumstance, viz., the cleric involved was recalcitrant about seeking pardon. The same statutes also decreed that a cleric who fomented schism in the Church was to be removed from his rank.[7] Once more it was troublemaking and the giving of scandal that served as warranting reasons for the removal of the delinquent cleric from his rank.

In Pontus, a council held at Neocaesarea (314-325) exemplified the similarity of legislation which, then extant in the East, dealt with clerics who were guilty of scandalous conduct or who were obdurate in their crime. The first canon of that council laid down the rule that a priest who married (i.e., after ordination) was to be deposed from his order.[8] Deposition was likewise decreed by the Council of Antioch in Syria (341) for any cleric who dared to continue using the computation of the Jews in the celebration of Easter after that synod had laid down its ruling in the matter. The reasons for inflicting this severe penalty were explicitly stated

[5] Canon 13—Bruns, II, 109; Hardouin, I, 265; Mansi, II, 472.

[6] Canon 57—Bruns, I, 147; Hardouin, I, 982.

[7] Canon 105—Bruns, I, 151; Hardouin, I, 986.

[8] Canon 1—Bruns, I, 71; Hardouin, I, 281; Mansi, II, 540.

as contumacy and the giving of scandal by the cleric.[9] This same council legislated that a priest or a deacon who *persistently* refused the behest of his bishop to return to his own church should likewise be deposed.[10] The same punishment was levied against a priest or a deacon who, *even after repeated warnings on the part of his bishop,* separated himself from his church, gathered his own coterie about him, and erected an altar.[11]

The Canons of the Apostles[12] imposed the same penalty on any bishop or priest who was negligent in the teaching of religion and *stubbornly persisted* in such negligence and sloth;[13] likewise on any bishop or priest who *would not be persuaded* to busy himself with Church matters, forsaking public business.[14] The same penalty was extended to include any deacons as well who dismissed their legitimate wives on the pretext of religion and *obstinately refused* to take them back;[15] or who were given to drunkenness and gambling, and *did not desist;*[16] or who *persistently* practiced usury in exacting debts owed to them;[17] or who *habitually* failed to render aid when a fellow member of the clergy was in need.[18] Canon 50 of the same collection inflicted the same penalty on any cleric who abstained from marriage, meat, or wine, not for the performance of any penance, but because he considered these things as abominations and *refused* to amend his ways.[19] Canon 54 also deposed any cleric who treated his bishop in an insolent fashion contrary to Scripture.[20]

---

[9] Canon 1—Bruns, I, 80; Hardouin, I, 594; Mansi, II, 1307.

[10] Canon 3—Bruns, I, 81; Hardouin, I, 593; Mansi, II, 1310.

[11] Canon 5—Bruns, I, 82; Hardouin, I, 595; Mansi, II, 1310.

[12] Most modern authorities attribute this collection to the early fifth century. Cf., e.g., Lijdsman, *Introductio in Ius Canonicum* (2 vols., Hilversum in Hollandia, 1924-1929), I, 99; Van Hove, *Prolegomena,* n. 123. Hence their treatment at this point.

[13] Canon 57 (numbering of the canons is according to that of Gentianus Hervetus)—Hardouin, I, 9, sqq.; Mansi, I, 30, sqq.

[14] Canon 80.

[15] Canon 5.

[16] Canon 41.

[17] Canon 43.

[18] Canon 58.

[19] ". . . vel *corrigatur,* vel deponatur."

[20] Cf. also Exodus, XXII, 28, and Acts, XXIII, 6.

Canon 3 of the Council of Antioch (341), mentioned above, which decreed deposition for any priest or deacon who persistently refused the request of his bishop to return to his own church, was repeated in canon 14 of the *Pseudo-Apostolic Canons* and broadened to include all clerics. Canon 5 of the same council, which forbade any priest or deacon to separate himself from his own church and erect an altar for his own group of followers, was repeated in the thirtieth of the *Canons of the Apostles* with the added admonition that deposition was to follow only after a threefold warning.

As a final proof of the fact that deposition was the usual penalty inflicted in this period for incorrigibility, one may consider the action taken by the III Ecumenical Council, that of Ephesus in 431. This Council sanctioned deposition as the penalty for all bishops who refused to join in the condemnation it promulgated against the Nestorian heresy. In the synodal letter which preceded the canons of this Council, such incorrigibility on the part of bishops resulted in their deposition from all ecclesiastical communion and the deprivation of their priestly power.[21]

Section 2. The Effect of Deposition on the Clerical Privileges in This Period

Before one can determine the effect of deposition on the clerical privileges at this time, it is necessary to consider just what was meant by those clerical privileges, and to discover if possible at just what time in the history of the Church they came into being. The second title of the second book of the Code lists the clerical privileges as follows: (1) the *privilegium canonis* (canon 119), which protects a cleric from real injury by making such an injury to be a sacrilege; (2) the *privilegium fori* (canon 120), which apart from the requisite permission forbids the summoning of a cleric before a lay judge either as a defendant in a contentious cause or as accused in a criminal cause; (3) the *privilegium immunitatis* (canon 121), which renders clerics immune from military service and from all public civil offices which are incompatible with the clerical state; and (4) the *privilegium competentiae*

[21] Conc. Ephesinum, *Epistola Synodica*—Hardouin, I, 1622.

(canon 122), which permits a cleric when under obligation to satisfy his creditors to retain as much of his resources as, in the prudent judgment of an ecclesiastical judge, is necessary for his decent support, though there remains of course the obligation to satisfy his creditors as soon as possible.

A. Privilegium Canonis

Not all of these privileges, however, are of equal antiquity. The first mentioned, namely that of the canon, takes its origin as a general law only from the time of the II General Council of the Lateran (1139) and its famed fifteenth canon, "*Si quis suadente diabolo.*"[22] In the period under discussion there was no need for the Church to constitute such a privilege, since clerics were sufficiently protected from real injury by the provisions of Roman Law. In 398, for example, the Emperors Arcadius (395-408) and Honorius (395-423) decreed that anyone who injured a priest or a minister of the Catholic Church was to receive at the hands of the provincial authorities a capital sentence (not necessarily the death penalty).[23] Deposition, therefore, could not possibly have resulted in a loss of the *privilegium canonis* during the first five centuries. As to its influence in succeeding centuries, subsequent articles will tell the tale.[24]

B. Privilegium Fori

St. Paul had already paved the way for the institution of the second of these clerical privileges, viz., that of the forum, when he counseled the primitive Christians in general, not just members of the clergy, to settle their disputes before an ecclesiastical judge

---

[22] C. 29, C. XVII, q. 4; cf. also II General Council of the Lateran, canon 15—Mansi, XXI, 530; Coronata, *Institutiones Iuris Canonici, Introductio*: *Ius Publicum Ecclesiasticum* (3. ed., Rome: Marietti, 1948), p. 193, n. 147, 5 (hereafter cited as *Ius Publicum Ecclesiasticum*). For precedents, cf. Council of Rheims (1131), canon 13—Mansi, XXI, 461; Council of Clermont (1130), canon 10—*ibid.*, 439; and others as below, pp. 37-38.

[23] C. (1, 3) 10; translated in Scott, *The Civil Law* (17 vols. in 7, Cincinnati: The Central Trust Co., 1932), XII, 32; cf. also C. (1, 3) 3 and (1, 3) (33.6); Coronata, *loc. cit.*

[24] Cf. pp. 33-34; 37-42 in this chapter.

rather than a civil magistrate.[25] Such counsel indeed was well accommodated to the times in which Paul was living, an era in which the newborn Church was being sorely tried by persecution. Once peace was restored to the Church, however, the lay faithful no longer were forbidden to approach civil judges for a settlement of their grievances.[26] Nevertheless the practice, as introduced in earlier and unhappier days, of going before ecclesiastical tribunals continued on into the new era of peace with the approbation of the civil as well as the ecclesiastical authorities. Constantine himself issued two constitutions (312 and 331 or 333) permitting all the faithful to take their causes before ecclesiastical tribunals, even though the other party was unwilling.[27] It is related of the same emperor that he refused to pass judgment on a controversial discussion of certain bishops because he recognized and respected the judiciary power of the Church in the matter under question.[28] When the bishops at the I General Council of Nicaea (325) requested him to settle a dispute which had arisen among them, Constantine replied: "The Lord has made you priests and given you the power for judging us, and therefore we are rightly judged by you. But you cannot be judged by men."[29] In this reply, Constantine voiced what has always been the mind of the Church relative to the privileged status of her clergy (at least those in major orders), viz., that those whom the Church has chosen as leaders in its spiritual army are above being judged by those whom they have been chosen to lead. Rather, they were to be judged by their fellow clerics in ecclesiastical courts. Secular rulers did not always continue so liberal in their acceptance of the Church's teaching on the privileged forum. Since the purpose of this brief inquisition into the history of the privileged forum itself, however, is to ascertain whether or not such a privilege actually existed in the various chronological periods into which this chapter is divided,

---

[25] Cf. I Cor., V, 1-6; Coronata, *op. cit.*, p. 189, n. 147, 3.

[26] Cf. Wernz, *Ius Decretalium*, Tom. V, lib. 1, p. 229, n. 277; Coronata, *loc. cit.*

[27] Cc. 35 and 36, C. XI, q. 1.

[28] St. Augustine, *Ep. XLIII*, n. 20—*MPL*, XXXIII, 169.

[29] Rufinus (345-410), *Historia Ecclesiastica*, lib. X, cap. 2—*MPL*, XXI, 468.

so that as a result it could have been affected by the *canonical* penalty of deposition in those respective periods, the purpose will be served if one presents only the ecclesiastical legislation on the subject.[80] The Church has from earliest times regarded the clergy as possessing such a privilege, and has zealously resisted any attempt on the part of secular powers to abolish or curtail the institute. After the Emperor Gratian (375-383) had decreed in 376 that only contentious cases and minor offenses of clerics were to be tried before ecclesiastical tribunals, while their criminal trials were to take place only before the civil magistrates,[81] the III Council of Carthage (397) ruled that clerics be tried only by other clerics, and not by laymen.[82] Two years later the Emperor Honorius (395-423) abolished the restriction placed on the privileged forum by Gratian, and explicitly ordered that only before the bishop could suits be lodged against clerics.[83] In 451 the Council of Chalcedon legislated that clerics could not have recourse to secular courts without the consent of their bishop.[84] When Valentinian III (425-455) in the following year decreed that a cleric could be hailed before the civil court in either a contentious or a criminal cause, and enacted also other repressive measures,[85] the Councils of Angers (c. 454)[86] and of Vannes (465)[87] reiterated the teaching of the Council of Chalcedon. Several councils before the Council of Chalcedon had already laid down practically the same norms which that general council set down in the aforementioned canon.[88] Other examples of patristic

[80] For a history of the civil legislation on the *privilegium fori* consult Downs, *The Concept of Clerical Immunity,* Catholic University of America Canon Law Studies, n. 126 (Washington, D. C.: Catholic University of America Press, 1941), chapters 2-4 incl.; Wernz, *Ius Decretalium,* Tom. V, lib. 1, nn. 277-283 incl.; Coronata, *Ius Publicum Ecclesiasticum,* pp. 190-191, n. 147, 3b.

[81] C. Th. (16, 2) 23.

[82] Canon 8—Hardouin, I, 962.

[83] C. Th. (16, 2) 41; cf. also C. Th. (16, 11) 1.

[84] Canon 9—Hardouin, II, 606; c. 46, C. XI, q. 1.

[85] N. Val. (3, 34) pr.

[86] Canon 1—Hardouin, II, 778.

[87] Canon 2—Hardouin, II, 797.

[88] Cf., e.g., canon 9, III Council of Carthage (397)—Hardouin, I, 962; canon 19, Council of Mileve (416)—Hardouin, I, 1220; canon 31, Council of Arles (442)—Hardouin, II, 775

record, pontifical ordinance, and conciliar legislation on the subject may be found in any specialized treatment of the topic. The examples already cited furnish sufficient evidence that ecclesiastical legislation in the first five centuries recognized (nay more, strenuously defended) the existence of the *privilegium fori*. Consequently, if deposition in this period did result in a deprivation of the clerical privileges, the *privilegium fori* could have been one of the privileges thus affected. As to subsequent legislation (both secular and ecclesiastical) concerning the privileged forum, the writer will be content to state that the Church continued to vindicate for clerics their exemption from trial before secular tribunals in the face of fluctuating civil legislation that affected this privilege up to the time when Emperor Frederick II (1215-1250) on the occasion of his coronation (1220) as Emperor of the Holy Roman Empire granted a total exemption of clerics and their goods from the secular tribunals and thus secured the privilege in civil law.[39] During the centuries intervening between the time of Constantine and that of Frederick, the *privilegium fori* existed theoretically, though for all practical purposes it was not always respected by the civil authorities. Since 1220 the Church has continued to retain the privilege right down to the present, though in various places its binding force has been mitigated through special provisions of concordats and other privileges.

C. Privilegium Immunitatis

The *privilegium immunitatis* was also of an early origin. During the era of persecution certainly one could not expect to find that clerics were exempt from public duties by authority of the Roman Empire. Those first three centuries were ages in which the Church and its ministers were at best barely tolerated. With the advent of Constantine, however, clerics of the Catholic Church, in accordance with the liberties granted the pagan priests, were gradually exempted from the duty to undertake municipal offices,

---

[39] Cf. *Monumenta Germaniae Historica* (Hannoverae-Lipsiae-Berolini, 1826-), *Legum Sectio IV, Constitutiones et Acta Publica Imperatorum et Regum* (8 toms. in 17 parts), Tom. II (ed. L. Weiland, Hannoverae, 1896), n. 85, 1-5 (hereafter cited *MGH*).

trusteeships, guardianships, and all public functions, from military service, quartering of soldiers, and the other personal *munera sordida,* and in part also from personal taxation.[40] Thus the cleric's *privilegium immunitatis* appeared early enough in the Church's history to be included in any effect which deposition would have had on the clerical privileges in the period running from the first up to and including the fifth century. To retail the subsequent history of this privilege will not further the purpose of this dissertation; it suffices to state that the Church down through the succeeding centuries continued to vindicate this particular clerical privilege whenever any secular power threatened encroachment upon it.[41] Accordingly, the privilege existed from the third century onward, and the deposed cleric could have been deprived of it, if indeed one showed that deposition did actually cause such an effect.

D. Privilegium Competentiae

The *privilegium competentiae* strictly understood, according to Coronata, does not go back farther than the time of Gregory IX (1227-1241).[42] Gregory had been approached on behalf of an indigent cleric, a certain Odoardus, who had been excommunicated by the Archdeacon of Rheims, because he could not pay the debts he owed to several persons. Pope Gregory commanded that the excommunication be lifted, with the precaution, however, that Odoardus, if he were later able to do so, settle his debts. Coronata states that while this exemption primarily exonerated the debtor

[40] Cf., e.g., C. Th. (16, 2) 24 in reference to exemption from personal services. Coronata (*Ius Publicum Ecclesiasticum,* p. 188, fn. 2) attributes this law to the year 377. Cf. also C. Th. (16, 2) 2 in reference to exemption from curial offices in the year 319; Coronata, *loc. cit.*

[41] Cf., e.g., Acts of the III Council of Toledo (589) in c. 69, C. XII, q. 2; c. 3, *de immunitate ecclesiarum, coemeteriorum, et aliorum locorum religiosorum,* III, 23, in VI°; c. 3, *de censibus, exactionibus, et procurationibus,* III, 13, in Clem.; cc. 2, 4, 7, X, *de immunitate ecclesiarum, coemiterii, et rerum, ad eas pertinentium,* III, 49; c. 4, *de censibus, exactionibus, et procurationibus,* III, 20, in VI°; c. un., *de immunitate ecclesiarum,* III, 17, in Clem.; Conc. Trident., sess. XXV, *de ref.,* c. 20.

[42] C. 3, X, *de solutionibus,* III, 23; cf. Coronata, *Ius Publicum Ecclesiasticum,* p. 192, n. 147, 4.

from the excommunication incurred, it later was given a much wider interpretation by various authors and by the jurisprudence of the Roman Curia itself, on an analogy to a similar privilege granted to soldiers by Roman Law.[43] This interpretation, Coronata goes on to state, erroneous though it be, is held by almost all authors, and in practice is to be retained because it already has constituted a centenary custom.[44] Johannes Baptist Sägmüller (1860-1942), on the other hand, maintained that such a historical derivation constituted a very poor foundation for the privilege. Rather, he referred the origin of the privilege to custom and to an idea expressed in several canons, namely that a cleric should not be reduced to such a state that he would be compelled to earn his living in a manner unworthy of his calling.[45] Whatever its origin, one cannot be sure of its existence before the thirteenth century. Hence it will not be considered as being capable of loss through the infliction of deposition until a review is made of the ecclesiastical legislation of that period in history that stretches from the twelfth century to the Council of Trent. This will be the task of the third article of this chapter.

E. Conclusions

Because of the late appearance of the *privilegium canonis* and the *privilegium competentiae* in the history of the Church, only two of the clerical privileges, viz., the *privilegium fori* and the *privilegium immunitatis,* could possibly have been lost through the infliction of deposition in antiquity. As regards the former privilege, Augustine held that it was not lost when a cleric was

---

[43] Cf. the glossa to D. (42.18) 6, which argued that the same privilege as granted to soldiers should be recognized in the needy cleric's case, since he served as a *"miles coelestis militiae."* Cf. Coronata, *loc. cit.*

[44] Coronata, *loc. cit.*

[45] *Lehrbuch des katholischen Kirchenrechts* (4. ed., Vol. I, 4 fascicles, Freiburg im Breisgau, 1925-1934), I, part 3, p. 354 (hereafter cited as *Lehrbuch*). Coronata, while differing as to the historical origin of the privilege, agrees that this is its *raison d'être* and notes that the present Code (canon 122) in retaining the privilege adduces the same reason for so doing.—Coronata, *loc. cit.*

deposed.[46] From the general tenor of medieval decretal legislation on the subject if appears that Augustine is correct. It was precisely because of the fact that the deposed cleric retained his *privilegium fori* that complaints about the abuse of the privileged forum arose, complaints which in turn occasioned the ultimate distinction between deposition and degradation in the Middle Ages.[47] The history of the legislation which led to that distinction will be treated in article three of the present chapter. Whether or not one subscribes to this opinion, however, it would not be amiss to point out here that, while deposition did not result in a loss of the *privilegium fori* for the first twelve centuries, in so far as the cleric retained his right to be tried only before an ecclesiastical tribunal, nevertheless civil legislation both in the Roman and Carolingian Empires often gave the state the power to inflict the punishment once a cleric had been deposed for certain crimes by an ecclesiastical tribunal.[48] Thus one finds the Council of Antioch (341), for example, decreeing that a priest or a deacon, if he had been deposed for separating himself from his church and setting up an altar for his followers, was to be punished by the secular authority (*per externam potentiam*) if he remained incorrigible even after being deposed.[49] There remains for consideration here only the effect of deposition on the *privilegium im-*

---

[46] Cf. *Commentary,* VIII, 259, fn. 12; cf. c. 10, X, *de iudiciis,* II, 1; c. 7, X, *de crimine falsi,* V, 20; c. 27, X, *de verborum significatione,* V, 40. There exists a vast literature on the subject, especially with regard to the dispute between St. Thomas, Archbishop of Canterbury (1162-1170) and King Henry II (1154-1189) in England. For a recent treatment, cf. Faveville, *L'église et la royante en Angleterre* (Paris, 1944). *Historically,* it is doubtful whether St. Thomas was in the right.

[47] Cf. Kober, *Die Deposition und Degradation,* p. 147; Wernz, *Ius Decretalium,* VI, n. 119; Findlay, *Deposition and Degradation,* pp. 66-72; Sweeney, *The Reduction of Clerics to the Lay State,* Catholic University of America Canon Law Studies, n. 223 (Washington, D. C.: Catholic University of America Press, 1945), pp. 5 and 6.

[48] Cf., e.g., N. CXXXVII, 4, and N. CXXIII (21, 1) in the Roman Law, and cap. 30, Synod of Frankfort (794), in the reign of Charlemagne—*MGH, Legum Sectio III, Concilia* (2 toms. in 3 parts with suppl.), Tom. II, pars prior, *Concilia Aevi Karolini* (recensuit Albertus Werminghoff, Hannoverae-Lipsiae: impensis Bibliopolii Hahniani, 1904), p. 169.

[49] Canon 5—Bruns, I, 82; Hardouin, I, 595; Mansi, II, 1310.

munitatis. Deposition in this period did result in the deprivation of the *privilegium immunitatis* of the deposed cleric, for there is evidence of such an effect in the civil legislation of the period. When the Roman Empire was at the height of its power and influence, offices in the *curia,* or also in the municipal government, were esteemed as honors and eagerly sought after. Once the Empire started to decline, however, more and more financial burdens were imposed upon the *curia* with the result that curial offices became positions which were anything but desirable.[50] As a result of the small number of volunteers, some means to provide incumbents for the various curial offices had to be found. Accordingly, in 408 there was issued by the Emperors Honorius and Arcadius a decree which authorized the *curia* to claim deposed clerics for its offices.[51] Hence one may deduce that of the four clerical privileges a deposed cleric up to the beginning of the sixth century sustained the loss of the *privilegium immunitatis* alone. With this observation in mind one can properly evaluate some of the canons of antiquity which speak of deposition as resulting in a loss of the clerical privileges. Either the *privilegium immunitatis* alone is meant, or simply certain extrinsic privileges (such as a special place in liturgical functions and various titles of honor and reverence) enjoyed because of some office, benefice, dignity, or pension which the deposed cleric had possessed as an individual, and not exclusively in virtue of the clerical state to which he belonged. It is to the latter species of clerical privilege that the Council of Antioch referred when it spoke of deposed clerics being deprived of the external honors to which they were entitled in virtue of the holy canon and the priesthood of God.[52]

---

[50] Cf. Jolowicz, *Historical Introduction to the Study of Roman Law* (Cambridge: University Press, 1932), pp. 357-358; Boak, *A History of Rome to 565 A. D.* (2. ed., New York: The Macmillan Co., 1938), pp. 309 and 371; Stephenson, *Medieval History* (New York: Harper and Bros., 1935), p. 26.

[51] C. Th. (16, 2) 39; cf. Gothofredus, *Commentarium in Codicem Theodosianum* (16, 2), 39.

[52] Canon 1—Hardouin, I, 594. For a discussion of what the "holy canon" was, cf. Bingham, *Antiquities,* I, 115. Briefly, it was a register which in each church contained the names of all the clergy. The Council of Nicaea

Section 3. Effect of Deposition on the Deposed Cleric's Revenue

The legislation of the Code provides that, if a deposed cleric be truly in need as a result of his deposition, the ordinary is bound in charity to provide for such a cleric in whatever manner he (the ordinary) deems most suitable, lest the deposed cleric be constrained to beg with consequent debasement redounding to the clerical state.[53] In the very next canon, however, it is stated that a deposed cleric who has been perpetually deprived of his right to wear the clerical garb according to due process of law is not to benefit from the aforementioned provision.[54] In antiquity clerics were supported from a central fund administered by the bishop.[55] Deposed clerics, however, were not entitled to a share in this fund.[56] Proof of this latter fact is supplied in the writings of St. Cyprian. In the case of certain subdeacons who had been deposed, Cyprian declared that they were not to share in the monthly distributions until their case had been decided.[57] A similar case occurred at Antioch in the year 268. Paul of Samosata, Patriarch of Antioch (260-268), was deposed as bishop of that See in that year, and Domnus (+272) was named as his successor in office. Paul, however, relying on the support of Zenobia, the secular ruler of Antioch, refused to leave the church or the rectory. Four years later, when Antioch was returned to the rule of Rome under the Emperor Aurelian (270-275), church authorities once more attempted to oust Paul from the See. Aurelian decided that Paul was ruling the See illegitimately (and consequently was not entitled to the fruits of the See), since the bishop of Antioch could only be he whom the Bishop of Rome recognized as such.[58] Two centuries later, another bishop of the same See

---

(325) legislated that a deposed cleric's name was to be taken from this list (canon 17—Hardouin, I, 330), and this removal resulted in a deprivation of all clerical honors and privileges. Cf. Wernz, *Ius Decretalium,* II, n. 233, p. 336.

[53] Canon 2303, § 2.

[54] Canon 2304, § 2.

[55] Cf. Bingham, *Antiquities,* I, 191.

[56] Cf. Hinschius, *Kirchenrecht,* IV, 726.

[57] *Ep. XXVIII—MPL,* IV, 302.

[58] Hughes, *A History of the Church* (New York: Sheed and Ward, 1935), I, 166.

(Domnus II [441-449]), less adamant than Paul, was deposed from his office. In that case the deposed bishop's successor, Maximus (449-455), besought the fathers of the Council of Chalcedon to have pity on his deposed predecessor, and to grant him some form of income, in which request the fathers of the Council acquiesced.[59] It should be noted that this concession of revenue to the deposed bishop by the members of the Council proceeded from their spirit of Christian charity, and not from any right in justice which the deposed bishop had. The regulation of canon 2303, § 2, is particularly parallel in its provision.

From these few examples one may conclude with a good deal of probability that, just as present canonical legislation exempts the ordinary from this obligation in charity towards deposed clerics once they have been deprived perpetually of their right to wear the garb, so too ecclesiastical legislation of the first five centuries most probably abolished an equivalent obligation in charity towards a deposed cleric, as imposed on bishops of that time, if the deposed cleric continued to give scandal and refused to amend even after deposition.

ARTICLE 2. DEPRIVATION OF THE CLERICAL GARB AS IMPLICIT IN DEPOSITION FROM THE SIXTH TO THE TWELFTH CENTURY

Section 1. Deposition as a Penalty for the Giving of Scandal and Incorrigibility

During this period from the sixth to the twelfth century, deposition continued to be inflicted as the ordinary penalty for the giving of scandal and for incorrigibility, much as it had been in the preceding centuries. But a difficulty arose from the fact that the clergy had commenced to wear as their ordinary dress a distinctive garb which singled them out from laymen. Clerics of the first five centuries, if they were scandalous in their behavior and recalcitrant about rectifying the bad example given, could be deposed and the situation was remedied once and for all. In the preceding article it was shown that deposition at that time deprived the deposed cleric of any immunities which he had pos-

[59] Acts of the Council of Chalcedon—Hardouin, II, 544.

sessed as a cleric, allowed him to be punished by the secular arm, and removed from him his right to any ecclesiastical income. Since he wore no special garb, the remedy was complete; the cleric might go on giving scandal, but there was at least no external evidence that he was a cleric. About the beginning of the sixth century, however, the Church perceived the need for some additional disciplinary measure. Deposition still achieved the above mentioned effects, but now even after deposition there still remained one indisputable bit of evidence that this person who was conducting himself in such a scandalous fashion was a member of the clergy, viz., the fact that he was clad in the clerical garb. In chapter one, article seven, of this dissertation it was stated that the cleric's ordinary garb most probably was removed along with his sacred vestments when deposition was inflicted in the centuries now under discussion. Several examples were cited there as proof of the fact that some sort of ceremony was always observed when this penalty was inflicted. Likewise it was remarked then that Pope Boniface VIII, when he explicitly commanded that the cleric's ordinary garb as well as his sacred vesture he denied him, because of the somewhat incidental manner in which he spoke of the former, was hardly introducing some new practice in the law. Thus it was concluded that prior to the time of Boniface, deprivation of the cleric's ordinary garb had for some period of time been implicit in the explicit deprivation of the cleric's sacred vestments effected by deposition. If this presumption were capable of apodictic proof as far back as the late fifth century, then no further proof would be required that deposition managed to offset scandalous clerical conduct down to the last detail, for in virtue of this presumption deposition would have effaced the last shred of evidence that the one giving scandal was indeed a member of the clerical state, namely, the evidence given by the miscreant's distinctive garb. Such, however, is not the case. The presumption remains just that and achieves nothing more; as such it can be impugned by historical evidence to the contrary. Historical evidence of such a nature does appear in canonical texts of the early sixth century. Starting with the Council of Agde (506) one finds relegation of the deposed cleric to a monastery appearing in canons of various councils as a legal consequence of deposition.[60] This additional effect of deposition could ensure the prevention of further scandal without necessitating a deprivation of the cleric's distinctive garb. Thus the hypothesis that deprivation of the cleric's ordinary garb in these centuries was implicit in deposition must be amended. It seems more correct to say that the prevention of further scandal by the deposed cleric was implemented in one of two ways, that is, either by deprivation of his distinctive garb (which deprivation was implicit in the legislation explicitly providing deprivation of the cleric's sacred vestments) or by relegating the deposed cleric to the seclusion of a monastery, while permitting him to retain and wear his distinctive garb. Of these two remedies, the existence of the former must remain in the realm of possibility. Enough has already been said and sufficient examples cited at the end of chapter one in support of the credibility of such a hypothesis. In addition, though it be admitted that the secluding of the cleric in a monastery obtained as a generally applicable penalty after the sixth century,[61] still room must be allowed for exceptions to the rule. What procedure was to be followed for the preventing of further scandal, for instance, if the deposed cleric (whose recalcitrance it must be remembered was one of the reasons why deposition was inflicted in the first place) continued obdurate even as to his ordered confinement in a monastery? Or again, what was to be done with a deposed cleric when no monastery was available for such an involuntary seclusion? Such cases were certainly within the realm of the possible and could present serious difficulties if relegation to a monastery had been the only means available to legitimate authority for the effective curbing of any continued scandal on the part of deposed clerics. Indeed, the Council of Chalon-sûr-Saone (813) envisioned just such a case. That council ruled that deposed clerics should be sent to a monastery for the performance of penance, but there was also the added admonition that, if this ruling proved impossible of observance, then those who were deposed were definitely not relieved of doing penance. Furthermore, when these latter circumstances obtained, then the

---

[60] Canon 20—Hardouin, II, 1003; c. 7, D.L.

[61] Cf. Benedictus XIV, *De synodo dioecesana,* lib. IX, c. 6, n. 3.

deposed clerics who neglected to do such penance and continued instead to live in a worldly fashion were to be punished further with excommunication.[62] In such a case, deprivation of the cleric's garb seemed to remain the sole means for the sure forestalling of further possible scandal.

As to the other method (confinement in a monastery) by which protracted scandal was quashed, there is abundant evidence in the legislation of the period. The above mentioned Council of Agde (506), for example, decreed this added punishment in the case of deposed bishops, priests, or deacons who had been guilty of perpetrating a capital crime, or of falsifying documents, or of committing perjury.[63] The III Council of Orleans (538) proclaimed the same added penalty for clerics deposed on the score of adultery.[64] A synod convened in Northern England early in the sixth century decreed a similar punishment for clerics deposed because of sins of the flesh.[65] Other numerous examples of similar legislation occur in the writings of the Popes and in the canons of the councils down through succeeding centuries even as far as the reign of Pope Innocent III (1198-1216) at the end of the twelfth century.[66]

Proof of the fact that deposition (coupled with either one of the two supplementary measures against further scandal) continued as the principal penalty in this period for the punishment

[62] Canon 40—Hardouin, IV, 1038; c. 8, D. LXXXI.

[63] Canon 50—Hardouin, II, 1003; c. 7, D. L. The Council of Epâon (517) decreed practically the same thing in its twenty-second canon.—*MGH, Legum Sectio III, Concilia,* Tomus I, *Concilia Aevi Merovingici* (resensuit Fridericus Maassen, Hanoverae: impensis Bibliopolii Hahniani, 1893), p. 24.

[64] Canon 7 (8?)—Hardouin, II, 1425; *MGH, ibid.,* p. 76.

[65] Cited by McNeill-Gamer, *Medieval Handbooks of Penance,* a translation of the principal *libri poenitentiales* and selections from related documents, Department of History, Columbia University: Records of Civilization, Sources and Studies, n. XXIX (New York: Columbia University Press, 1938), p. 170 (hereafter cited as *Penitentials*).

[66] Cf., e.g., Epistles of St. Gregory the Great, *Ep. XXVII,* Epist. lib. III—*MGH, Epistolarum Sectio* (7 toms. in 11 parts), Toms. I et II in 4 parts, *Gregorii I Papae Registrum Epistolarum* (ediderunt P. Ewald et L. Hartmann, Berolini: apud Weidmannos, 1891-1899), Tom. I, part 1, p. 185; canon 29 of the IV Council of Toledo (633)—Hardouin, III, 586; c. 10, X, *de purgatione canonica,* V, 34.

of scandal and of incorrigibility on the part of clerics may be inferred from the abundant disciplinary measures taken against clerics who when violating the law of clerical celibacy gave grave scandal. The first written law on this matter had been promulgated in the West by the Council of Elvira (ca. 306) and in the East by the Council of Ancyra (314).[67] Now, two centuries later, Pope John II (533-535), having learned that Contumeliosus, Bishop of Riez, had been sentenced by the Council of Marseilles (533) to do penance in a monastery because he had committed adultery, stated that Contumeliosus was not only to be relegated to a monastery but also to be deposed in accordance with the decrees of the older canons.[68] In 538 a deposition for all clerics in major orders who violated the law of celibacy was decreed by the III Council of Orleans.[69] The V Council of Orleans, only eleven years later, reestablished perpetual deposition for all violators of clerical celibacy.[70] In the following century, the VIII Council of Toledo (653) declared that bishops who were found wanting in the virtue of priestly chastity were to be punished with the irrevocable sentence of the fathers, i.e., with deprivation of the dignity of their rank and order.[71] Other crimes in which the elements of scandal and incorrigibility were inherent likewise called for the penalty of deposition. The Penitential of Theodore of Canterbury (668-690), for example, though not an official source of the prevailing discipline, imposed deposition on any ordained person who was habitually addicted to the vice of drunkenness and would not amend;[72] on any priest who, because of the inconvenience necessitated by a journey, refused to baptize

---

[67] Canon 33 of the Council of Elvira—Mansi, II, 11; canon 10 of the Council of Ancyra—Mansi, II, 518.

[68] *Ep. Ioannis Papae II*—Hardouin, II, 1156; Jaffé, *Regesta Pontificum Romanorum ab condita Ecclesia ad annum post Christum natum 1198* (2. ed. correctam et auctam auspiciis Gulielmi Wattenbach curaverunt S. Loewenfeld, F. Kaltenbrunner, P. Ewald, 2 vols. in 1, Lipsiae, 1885-1888), JK, n. 886 (hereafter cited as JL, JK, or JE, with the corresponding number of the document).

[69] Canon 2—Hardouin, II, 1425.

[70] Canon 4—Hardouin, II, 1444.

[71] Canon 4—Hardouin, III, 962.

[72] Book I, tit. 1, canon 1—McNeill, *Penitentials*, p. 184.

a person in danger of death with the result that the sick person died without baptism;[73] on a cleric guilty of murder or fornication;[74] and on a bishop, priest, or deacon, guilty of fornication.[75]

In eighth-century England a work appeared under the name of Archbishop Egbert of York (735-766) entitled the *Dialogue of Egbert* (c. 750). In it was to be found a series of questions, the fifteenth of which raised the query: "What are the crimes which prevent any man from becoming a priest, or for what (offenses) is one deposed who has already been ordained?" In the answer to this question are listed several crimes involving the element of scandal, e.g., the worshipping of idols; the giving of one's self over to the devil through the medium of soothsayers, diviners, and enchanters; the commission of murder or fornication.[76] Other sources, both official and unofficial, repeat the same doctrine all through the period. Those here cited are proof sufficient for the contention made.

Section 2. Effect of Deposition on the Clerical Privileges in This Period

A. Privilegium Canonis

In the previous article it was pointed out that the *privilegium canonis* as such did not exist in the first five centuries of the Church's history. Consequently, it could not have been lost when a cleric was deposed. After the period of Christian antiquity had passed, however, a gradual need became apparent for the enactment of punishments in order that clerics might be safeguarded against real injury. The Roman Empire had been overrun by the barbarian hordes with a consequent loss of the protective measures afforded by Roman Law. Accordingly, laws began to be enacted by various particular councils and by some of the Popes for particular territories with a view to the protection of clerics from real injury. Pope Nicholas I (858-867), for example, wrote to the Archbishop of Milan that those who inflicted corporal punishment on clerics were to be excommunicated if they

[73] Book I, title IX, canon 7—McNeill, *op. cit.*, p. 193.

[74] Book I, title IX, canon 8—McNeill, *loc. cit.*

[75] Book I, title IX, canon 1—McNeill, *op. cit.*, p. 192.

[76] McNeill, *op. cit.*, p. 239.

failed to amend after three warnings.[77] The Synod of Rome (862 or 863) legislated that a person striking, beating, or killing a bishop incurred excommunication.[78] The Council of Ravenna (877) enacted that anyone who wrought an injury on an ecclesiastical person would upon a due previous warning be deprived of communion until he had made the reparation required by law. If after a second and third warning he was still manifestly unwilling to make satisfaction, he was to be regarded as courting even the crime of sacrilege.[79] Alexander II (1061-1073) ruled that anyone who arrested, struck, or forcefully expelled from his office any cleric, without that cleric's having been canonically judged, was to be subjected to canonical penance and deposition. If he proved obdurate, he was to be excommunicated.[80]

Thus it is evident that the Church during this whole period was perceptibly tending to the establishment of what was later to be known as the *privilegium canonis.* The culmination of all this particular legislation was to come about as the result of the anticlerical heresies which sprang up in the early twelfth century. This phase of the development of the *privilegium canonis* will receive treatment in the ensuing article, which deals with the period extending from the twelfth century to the Council of Trent. It will be sufficient here to note that deposition at the time under discussion in the present article could not possibly have resulted in the loss of that privilege.

B. Privilegium Fori

As to the correlation of deposition and the *privilegium fori,* an interesting development may be noted in the period under dis-

[77] C. 23, C. XVII, q. 4; JE, n. 2864.

[78] Canon 14—Mansi, XV, 660; cf. Sägmüller, *Lehrbuch,* I, 335, who maintains that the penalty here enacted was incurred *ipso facto.* McGrath (*The Privilege of the Canon,* The Catholic University of America Canon Law Studies, n. 242 [Washington, D. C.: Catholic University of America Press 1946], p. 13, fn. 5) states that the wording of the canon itself militates against Sägmüller's interpretation.

[79] Canon 5—Mansi, XVII, 338.

[80] C. 22, § 1, C. XVII, q. 4. Some authors attribute this legislation to canon 3 of the VIII Synod of Constantinople held under Photius; cf. Coronata, *Ius Publicum Ecclesiasticum,* p. 193, fn. 3.

cussion. It has already been stated that deposition did not result in a loss of this privilege until after the twelfth century. At the same time it was stated that the deposed cleric's retention of this privilege did not preclude the possibility of his being handed over to the secular court for the infliction of punishment. After he had been tried, found guilty, and been deposed by an ecclesiastical tribunal, civil laws often provided that he should be relinquished to the secular arm for punishment. Similar procedure began to creep into ecclesiastical legislation with the appearance of the Pseudo-Isidorian decretals in the ninth century.[81] Among these decretals, purporting to be genuine ecclesiastical legislation, were three decretals attributed therein to three popes of the first three centuries: Pius I (142-157), Fabian I (236-250), and Stephen I (254-257). Provision was made in all three for transmission to the *curia* of any cleric deposed because of disobedience, treachery, insults, etc., towards his bishop.[82] Three centuries later, Gratian incorporated all three of these spurious decretals in his *Decree* (c. 1140).[83] It is apparent from his dictum after the second of the three, that Gratian interpreted these phrases which mentioned delivery to the *curia* as signifying that the deposed cleric was to be delivered to the *curia* in order to receive that body's judgment.[84] If such a delivery of the cleric had been undertaken, then indeed the deposed cleric would have suffered a loss of his *privilegium fori* as a result of his deposition even as early as the second century. The truth of the matter, however, was that the forger of the Pseudo-Isidorian Decretals,

[81] The time and place of composition of this largely spurious collection has been designated by most modern authorities as lying somewhere between the years 847-857 in the province of Tours or in the city of Rheims; cf. Van Hove, *Prolegomena,* n. 164. A critical reading of the text is available in Hinschius, *Decretales Pseudo-Isidorianae et Capitula Angilramni* (Lipsiae, 1863), which work will hereafter be cited as *Decretales Pseudo-Isidorianae.*

[82] For the decretal attributed to Pius I, cf. *Ep. II,* c. 10—*Hinschius, Decretales Pseudo-Isidorianae,* p. 120; for that assigned to Fabian I, cf. *Ep. II,* c. 21—Hinschius, *op. cit.,* p. 165; for that attributed to Stephen I, cf. *Ep. II,* c. 12—Hinschius, *op. cit.,* p. 186.

[83] Cf. c. 18, C. XI, q. 1; c. 31, C. XI, q. 1; and c. 8, C. III, q. 4, respectively.

[84] Cf. *Dictum Gratiani* following c. 31, C. XI, q. 1.

whoever he was, had presented legislation of the Roman Civil Law in the guise of ecclesiastical legislation emanating from these particular Popes. Hinschius (1835-1898) pointed out that the expression *curiae tradere* in all three was not derived from ecclesiastical legislation at all, but rather from the imperial constitution issued in 408 by Arcadius and Honorius, already cited in the preceding article with its correct interpretation in reference to the deposed cleric's loss of the *privilegium immunitatis.*[85] This original meaning of the phrase was not known to canonists contemporaneous with or also immediately subsequent to the time of Gratian (+ ca. 1157). Ignorant of the legislation of antiquity, and relying instead on the authority of Pseudo-Isidore and Gratian himself, they interpreted the phrase as an endorsement by ecclesiastical legislation of the practice of handing over deposed clerics to secular tribunals for punishment.[86] Such procedure of course demanded a reduction of the cleric to the lay state, including the loss of his *privilegium fori.* Moreover, the *Decree of Gratian,* while never officially recognized as authentic, exerted such a profound influence on subsequent authentic ecclesiastical legislation that this erroneous interpretation gradually crept into authentic church law, and finally was given a definite legal signification therein by Pope Innocent III in 1209. This latter development will receive fuller consideration in the next article, wherein the ecclesiastical legislation from the twelfth century to the Council of Trent is treated.

Section 3. Effect of Deposition on the Deposed Cleric's Revenue

Just as deposition in antiquity had resulted in the deposed cleric's loss of any right to share in the distribution of the central church fund by the bishop, so too the same penalty continued to exert a detrimental effect on the deposed cleric's revenue in this period. The III Council of Orleans (538), for example, declared that any cleric who refused to fulfill the obligations of his office, or to show the proper respect and obedience owing to his bishop, was not to be numbered with the canonical clerics nor like them

---

[85] *Decretales Pseudo-Isidorianae,* pp. 120, 165, and 185.

[86] Cf. Baronius, *Annales Ecclesiastici,* XIX (an. 1164), 230.

to be given any means of support from church funds.[87] Worthy of note here again is the fact that the deposition which resulted in the loss of ecclesiastical support for the deposed clerics was itself the result of scandalous conduct and incorrigibility. Pope Gregory the Great (590-604) in one of his many epistles likewise furnished implicit evidence that deposition deprived the deposed cleric of his right to the help of support. The case in question involved a certain deposed priest by the name of Marcellus, who had been confined to a monastery for the performance of penance. Gregory commanded that the necessities of life be provided for him, implying that Marcellus had no other means of support save the means afforded by the monks' exercise of Christian charity.[88] As with reference to the legislation presented by antiquity, one may again conclude with probability here in this period that this obligation in charity towards the deposed cleric no longer bound ecclesiastical authorities, once the former by his continued bad example showed himself unworthy of their charity.

ARTICLE 3. DEPRIVATION OF THE CLERICAL GARB AS EXPLICIT IN ACTUAL DEGRADATION FROM THE TWELFTH CENTURY TO THE COUNCIL OF TRENT

Section 1. Proximate Evolution of the Privilegium Canonis

It has already been pointed out how deposition could not possibly have resulted in a loss of the *privilegium canonis* for the first eleven centuries. With the beginning of the twelfth century, however, there arose in the history of the Church a new developmnt which demanded a severer ecclesiastical discipline in regard to the safeguarding of clerics and the honor due their state. At the instigation of certain heretics, such as Arnold of Brescia (ca. 1100-1155), imbued with anticlerical tendencies, clerics and religious alike were being subjected to intolerable abuses. These excesses were made even worse when one considers that clerics and religious were forbidden by law to carry weapons with which

---

[87] Canon 11—Hardouin, II, 1425.

[88] *Ep. XVIII (ad Petrum Subdiaconum)*, Epist. lib. I—*MPL*, LXXVII, 463.

to defend themselves.[89] Because of this alarming tendency, Pope Urban II (1088-1099) had already in 1095 at the Council of Clermont established excommunication as the punishment for those who laid violent hands on clerics.[90] It seems as if this punishment was not universally accepted, for in 1130 one finds Pope Innocent II (1130-1143) renewing the same penalty at the Synod of Clermont.[91] The Council of Rheims renewed the penalty just one year later.[92] Again, in 1135, the Council of Pisa reestablished the same sanction.[93] Finally the punishment was given worldwide binding force by the II General Council of the Lateran (1139) in its well known fifteenth canon; "Item placuit ut si quis suadente diabolo . . . etc."[94] A study of the further history of this privilege will be of no benefit to the purpose of this study. It has been established that the privilege as such did not exist before the twelfth century. After that time it remained essentially the same, suffering only minor accidental revision. Wherefore, from the early twelfth century on, the *privilegium canonis* was an actuality along with the other clerical privileges and could have been lost as a result of deposition if that penalty entailed such a deprivation after that time. Hence a discussion of whether or not such an effect really occurred is in order. A study of the medieval legislation which led gradually to a distinction between deposition and degradation as two separate penalties will show that, once this distinction had been made, degradation alone entailed such an effect.

Section 2. Effect of Medieval Distinction Between Deposition and Degradation on the Clerical Privileges

In the preceding articles it has been pointed out that ecclesiastical legislation in the first twelve centuries did not deprive a

[89] Cf. Coronata, *Ius Publicum Ecclesiasticum,* p. 193, n. 147, 5°; McGrath, *The Privilege of the Canon,* pp. 18 and 20.

[90] Canon 32—Hefele-Leclercq, *Histoire des Conciles* (11 vols. in 20, Paris: Librairie Letouzey et Ané, 1907-1949), V, 455.

[91] Canon 10—Mansi, XXI, 439; Hinschius, *Kirchenrecht,* I, 118.

[92] Canon 13—Mansi, XXI, 461.

[93] Canon 12—Mansi, XXI, 490.

[94] C. 29, C. XVII, q. 4; Mansi, XXI, 530.

cleric of his right to the privileged forum once he had been deposed. In the face of fluctuating civil legislation on the matter, the Church always maintained this right for clerics even in criminal causes.[95] Such an ironclad exemption, however, began to result in abuses on the part of some clerics with consequent complaints on the part of the laity.[96] The origin of these abuses can be explained from the fact that, since ecclesiastical discipline among its penalties forbade the infliction of capital punishment,[97] and since clerics were not subject to the secular discipline which did, there was not a sufficient deterrent to prevent clerics from committing certain grave crimes ordinarily punished in the secular courts with a capital sentence.[98] In order to remedy this abuse of the privileged forum by clerics and at the same time to remove any cause for complaint by the faithful, the Church, in the person of its Supreme Pontiffs, began to take steps which indeed maintained the privilege of the forum for the clergy in general, but denied it to clerics guilty of certain grave crimes.

As already noted, canonists contemporary with and immediately subsequent to Gratian, because of their unfamiliarity with the ecclesiastical legislation of antiquity, had begun to misinterpret the phrase *curiae tradere* as contained in Gratian's *Decree,* giving it the signification which the forger of the Pseudo-Isidorian decretals desired for it, namely that the deposed cleric was to be delivered to the secular court to receive the judgment of that body, rather than the true interpretation by which the phrase signified the cleric's loss of the right that exempted him from the burdensome offices of the *curia.*[99] Imbued with an erroneous interpretation of the phrase, and partly motivated by the desire to retrace the steps taken during the controversy between St. Thomas of Canterbury and King Henry II, several Supreme

[95] Cf., e.g., c. 4, X, *de iudiciis,* II, 1; *ibid.,* c. 8.

[96] Cf. Wernz, *Ius Decretalium,* VI, n. 119.

[97] C. 30, C. XXIII, q. 8; cc. 5, 9, X, *ne clerici vel monachi saecularibus negotiis se immisceant,* III, 50; cf. Fagnanus, *Commentaria in Quinque Libros Decretalium* (4 vols., Venetiis, 1697), lib. V, tit. 40, cap. 27, n. 8; hereafter cited as *Commentaria.*

[98] Kober, *Die Deposition und Degradation,* p. 147.

[99] Cf. Baronius, *Annales Ecclesiastici,* XIX (an. 1164), 230.

Pontiffs began to enact remedial legislation simultaneously curbing clerical abuses of the privileged forum and removing justifiable lay complaints. In 1184, Pope Lucius III (1181-1185) decreed that clerics who persisted in heresy, that is, who did not retract their errors and promise satisfaction, were to be stripped of their prerogatives of orders, and thus deprived of ecclesiastical offices and benefices were to be relinquished to the judgment of the secular power to be punished with an appropriate penalty.[100] Towards the close of the same century, Pope Celestine III (1191-1198) took another step towards the canonization in ecclesiastical law of this erroneous interpretation of the phrase *curia tradere*. This Pope had been asked whether or not it was licit for any secular judge to sentence clerics found guilty of theft, murder, perjury, or other crimes. He ruled that it was the task of an ecclesiastical tribunal to convict and depose such clerics. If after deposition these clerics still continued in their errant ways, they were to be excommunicated. If this latter penalty proved insufficient for breaking down the cleric's contumacy, anathemas were to be invoked against him. Then, and only then, if these clerics still remained incorrigible, and with a view to preventing further scandal and the possible damnation of many others, was the secular power to step in and inflict exile or some other serious penalty upon them.[101] While the legislation enacted by these two twelfth-century Popes implicitly set down the various elements necessary for a distinction between deposition and degradation as two separate penalties, the actual making of the distinction was left to the legislation of the great canonist Pope, Innocent III (1198-1216), in the following century. This great pope, striving to terminate the crime of forgery in general and the forgery of papal documents in particular, decreed in 1202 that clerics detected

---

[100] C. 9, X, *de haereticis*, V, 7. Devoti (1744-1820) held this enactment of Lucius to be the first ecclesiastical law allowing the secular court some power, albeit secondary and indirect, for inflicting punishment on a deposed cleric (cf. *Institutiones*, I, tit. IV, § 21, n. 2).

[101] C. 10, X, *de iudiciis*, II, 1. Benedict XIV (1740-1758) considered this ruling of Celestine's to be the introduction, or at least the first official recognition, in canon law of the distinction between deposition and degradation (cf. *De synodo dioecesana*, lib. IX, cap. 6, n. 3).

in this crime were to be deprived of all ecclesiastical offices and benefices *in perpetuum,* and that those who committed the actual crime of forgery were to be degraded by an ecclesiastical judge and then delivered to the secular power to be punished according to the lawful constitutions.[102] Thus the decree recognized two separate penalties in deposition and degradation. Clerics who co-operated in the falsification of papal letters were to be deposed; those who did the actual forging were to be degraded and turned over to the secular tribunal for punishment. Evidently the decree caused some controversy as to just what Innocent had meant when he said that degraded clerics were to be handed over to the secular court, for in 1209 Innocent found it necessary to render an official interpretation of the term *curiae tradere* as it was contained in the canons of antiquity and in his own decree establishing the penalty for clerical forgery. In so doing, he referred to the various interpretations formerly given the term and then canonized the interpretation which had sprung into prominence after the time of Pseudo-Isidore, namely, that a cleric degraded by the ecclesiastical court was thereby deprived of the clerical privileges, and in consequence was subject to the secular court.[103] All four of these decretals were later included by Pope Gregory IX (1227-1241) in his official collection and thus obtained universal binding force. Consequently, from this time on the two penalties must be recognized as distinct penalties, inflicted for their own specific reasons and producing their own peculiar effects.

Once Innocent III had succeeded in establishing a clear-cut distinction between the two penalties of deposition and degradation, the latter penalty alone entailed the loss of the clerical privileges. Deposition, serious as it was, left these privileges intact.[104] Degradation, on the other hand, did effect such a loss.[105] Bearing witness to the truth of this statement are the decretals of Lucius III, Celestine III, and Innocent III, already mentioned in relation to their bearing on the ultimate distinction of deposition and degradation as two separate penalties. The foregoing dis-

[102] C. 7, X, *de crimine falsi,* V, 20.

[103] C. 27, X, *de verborum significatione,* V, 40.

[104] Cf. Findlay, *Deposition and Degradation,* pp. 73, 75, 76, 85.

[105] Cf. Fagnanus, *Commentaria,* lib. II, tit. I, cap. 10, n. 16.

cussion suffices in regard to the effect of this distinction on the clerical privileges. Whether or not either of these penalties was inflicted for scandal and incorrigibility in this period will be the subject of the next section.

Section 3. Punishment of Scandal and Incorrigibility in This Period

During the period under discussion, clerics guilty of scandalous conduct and incorrigibility were punished sometimes with deposition, sometimes with degradation. The latter penalty was inflicted only for a limited number of specified crimes which were particularly grave in their nature. The earliest example of this penalty's infliction was its use as the punishment for the falsification of papal letters by Innocent III, as pointed out in the preceding section. Most frequently, however, it was invoked as the penalty for heresy and schism, both of which crimes obviously involved the elements of scandal and incorrigibility.[106] As a punishment for other grave crimes, degradation was inflicted only when a cleric already deposed for such crimes remained incorrigible.[107] An example of the latter case is evinced in the legislation of Pope Celestine III. That Pope sanctioned degradation as the penalty for those clerics who refused to amend their ways after their earlier deposition because of theft, murder, perjury, or other grave crimes.[108]

In addition to these three crimes, deposition was also decreed in this period for clerics guilty of simony, incest, sodomy, incorrigible concubinage, absolving and burying an impenitent sacrilegious thief, incorrigibility in acts of physical violence, repeated disobedience, and violating the seal of confession.[109] These

[106] For examples of degradation as the penalty for heresy, cf. cc. 9, 13, 15, X, *de haereticis,* V, 7; cc. 1, 2, *de haereticis,* V, 2 in VI°; Reiffenstuel, *Ius Canonicum Universum* (5 vols. in 6, Romae, 1831-1834), lib. V, tit. 37, n. 143; for examples of degradation as the penalty for schism, cf. c. 26, X, *de verborum significatione,* V, 40; c. un., *de schismaticis,* V, 3, in VI°.

[107] Cf. Schmalzgrueber, *Ius Ecclesiasticum Universum* (5 vols. in 12, Romae, 1843-1845), lib. V, tit. 37, n. 153.

[108] C. 10, X, *de iudiciis,* II, 1.

[109] Cf. c. 11, X, *de simonia, et ne aliquid pro spiritualibus exigatur vel promittatur,* V, 3; c. 15, X, *de purgatione canonica,* V, 34; cc. 4, 6, X, *de cohabitatione clericorum et mulierum,* III, 2; c. 2, X, *de raptoribus, in-*

and other crimes like them, when they involved scandal and incorrigibility, were all punished with deposition. Degradation, on the other hand, was employed as punishment only for a few specified crimes and for incorrigibility after deposition, when the reason for the deposition had been one of the more heinous crimes.

Section 4. Deprivation of the Clerical Garb as Explicit in Actual Degradation

It was in this period that Pope Boniface VIII explicitly stated that the deprivation of the cleric's ordinary garb, as well as the removal of his sacred vestments, was to accompany the infliction of the penalty of degradation. This explicit statement resulted from an inquiry by the Bishop of Béziers as to how the penalty of degradation was to be inflicted. The fact that degradation was a penalty distinct from deposition, as well as the consideration of the very nature of the former penalty, was clear enough from the legislation of Innocent III on the matter.[110] It was the legal procedure to be followed when inflicting the penalty that still caused some doubts. Accordingly, Boniface replied to the request of the Bishop of Béziers for further information by drawing a distinction between verbal degradation and real degradation. The former, which consisted in the pronouncement of a judicial sentence, was to be performed in the case of major clerics by the ordinary assisted by the number of bishops required by the canons; by the bishop alone, in the case of clerics in minor orders. The latter was to consist in the execution of that sentence through a solemn act of stripping from the delinquent all his clerical insignia, *including the degraded cleric's ordinary garb.* Once this had taken place, the cleric, bereft of his rank and privileges, no longer was considered as a member of the clergy.[111] Whereas in previous centuries the act of deposition was often accompanied

cendiariis et violatoribus ecclesiarum, V, 17; c. 1, X, *de clerico percussore,* V, 25; c. 15, X, *de excessibus praelatorum et subditorum,* V, 31; c. 12, X, *de paenitentiis et remissionibus,* V, 38.

[110] C. 7, X, *de crimine falsi,* V, 20; c. 27, X, *de verborum significatione,* V, 40.

[111] Cf. c. 2, *de poenis,* V, 9, in VI°.

with some form of ceremony expressive of the ignominy attaching to it,[112] it was juridically complete, nonetheless, simply with a pronunciation of the sentence.[113] Real degradation, on the other hand, required this solemn ceremony as an integral part.[114] Probably deprivation of the cleric's ordinary garb was explicit in the carrying out of actual degradation ever since the time of the decrees issued by Innocent III, since Boniface from the casual wording of his decree did not seem to be making any innovation. Indeed Durandus (1237-1296), in commenting on the two decrees of Innocent, bore out this supposition.[115] Since the procedure was doubtful even after the promulgation of those decretals, however, the decree of Boniface will be considered as the first definite proof of this fact. Accordingly, at least from the time of Boniface onward, deprivation of the cleric's ordinary garb will be considered as having been an explicit ceremony and integral part of the whole solemn ceremony proper to actual or real degradation.

ARTICLE 4. FROM THE COUNCIL OF TRENT TO THE ENACTMENT OF THE CODE OF CANON LAW

Section 1. Distinction Between Deposition and Verbal Degradation

As has been pointed out in the preceding article, the only difference between the penalty of deposition and that of actual degradation consisted in this, viz., that the latter deprived the delinquent cleric of all his clerical privileges, while the former left these privileges intact. This difference remains even today in the legislation of the Code.[116] What should be noted in the legislation of the Code, however, is that the deprivation of the clerical privileges is attributed directly to the perpetual deprivation of the clerical garb, and only indirectly to degradation, i.e., only in so far

---

[112] Cf. Martène, *De Antiquis Ecclesiae Ritibus,* lib. III, cap. 2.

[113] Cf. Durandus, *Speculum Iuris cum Ioannis Andreae, Baldi de Ubaldis aliorumque aliquot praestantissimorum Iurisconsultorum Theorematibus* (Venetiis, 1577), lib. III, partic. I, *de accusatione,* § 2, n. 4 (hereafter cited as *Speculum Iuris*).

[114] C. 27, X, *de verborum significatione,* V, 40; c. 2, *de poenis,* V, 9, in VI°.

[115] *Speculum Iuris, loc. cit.*

[116] Cf. canons 2303, § 1; 2304, § 2; 2305.

as the former is contained in the latter as a constitutive element.[117] The difficulty which presented itself in the period under discussion consisted in a placing of the proper interpretation on Pope Boniface's distinction between verbal and actual degradation. Some of the canonists of that time understood verbal degradation to be nothing more than deposition.[118] Others maintained a real distinction between the two.[119] This second opinion, which Chelodi (1880-1922) termed the more common one,[120] compared the distinction between verbal and actual degradation to that between the pronouncement of a judicial sentence and the execution of that sentence. It was only with the execution of the sentence, namely with the carrying out of the actual degradation in its solemn ceremony, that the cleric stood bereft of all his clerical privileges. Verbal degradation affected these privileges no more than did deposition.[121]

The reason why the penalty of verbal degradation was not to be identified with that of deposition lay precisely in the direct relationship which the former bore to actual degradation, which relationship was entirely lacking in the notion of deposition. Deposition was a penalty complete and entire in itself. One could not depose a cleric and then subject him to actual degradation. Verbal degradation had to intervene. Moreover, verbal degradation could be inflicted only for those crimes which warranted actual degradation, which certainly was not true of the penalty of deposition.[122] Consequently, from this time up to the enactment

---

[117] Cf. canons 2304, § 2; 2305, § 1.

[118] Cf., e.g., Fagnanus, *Commentaria,* lib. V, tit. 1, cap. 6, n. 76; Reiffenstuel, *Ius Canonicum Universum,* lib. V, tit. 37, nn. 22, 32; Barbosa, *Collectanea Doctorum tam Veterum quam Recentiorum in Ius Pontificium Universum* (2 vols., Lugduni, 1716), lib. V, tit. IX, in VI°, cap. 2, n. 4 (hereafter cited as *Collectanea*).

[119] Cf., e.g., Schmalzgrueber, *Ius Ecclesiasticum Universum,* lib. V, tit. 37, n. 138; Benedictus XIV, *De synodo dioecesana,* lib. IX, cap. 6, n. 3; Leurenius, *Ius Canonicum Universum* (5 vols. in 3, Venetiis, 1729), lib. V, tit. 37, q. 527.

[120] *Ius Poenale,* n. 53.

[121] Cf. Benedictus XIV, ep. encycl., *Quam grave,* 2 aug. 1757—*Fontes,* n. 443.

[122] Cf. Benedictus XIV, *loc. cit.*

of the Code, deprivation of the clerical garb should be considered as accompanying actual degradation alone, since actual degradation alone entailed the chief effect now ascribed to deprivation of the clerical garb, viz., the loss of the clerical privileges. Evidence of the truth of this statement can also be inferred from the fact that the charitable aid which the Code now prohibits to clerics deprived perpetually of their right to wear the clerical garb[123] was not so prohibited to *deposed* clerics in the period under discussion.[124]

Here one may well note with Vidal (1867-1938) that this distinction between verbal and actual degradation no longer obtains in the disciplinary legislation of the Code. Because of the practical difficulty involved in compelling a delinquent cleric to undergo the penalty of actual degradation, and because of the fact that perpetual deprivation of the clerical garb now removes the clerical privileges from the culprit, verbal and actual degradation now differ only in solemnity, both producing the peculiar effects formerly ascribed to actual degradation alone.[125]

Section 2. Punishment of Scandal and Incorrigibility

During this period from the Council of Trent to the enactment of the Code, the giving of scandal and incorrigibility on the part of delinquent clerics continued to be punished either with the penalty of deposition or with that of degradation. As to which of the two penalties was to be invoked in any given instance, custom and the practical application of penal laws in particular cases began to make their influence felt. While many laws enacted deposition as the penalty for a certain crime, there gradually appeared, at least in practice, certain restrictions which limited the infliction of deposition to certain more atrocious crimes. The Fathers of the Council of Trent themselves had supplied the precedent for this milder practice when they decreed that deposition was to be inflicted on clerics living in concubinage only after

---

[123] Cf canon 2304, § 2.

[124] Cf. Wernz, *Ius Decretalium,* VI, n. 125.

[125] Cf. Wernz-Vidal, *Ius Canonicum,* VII, n. 352; cf. also, *ibidem,* fn. 147; Wernz, *Ius Decretalium,* VI, n. 140.

such clerics had been warned several times and had shown themselves unmoved by the milder penalties first employed against them.[126] In a similar lenient vein, the same men had ruled in an earlier session of that Council that those who were *publicly* and *notoriously* stained with crime should not be permitted "to minister at the holy altar or to assist at the sacred services."[127]

With these two provisions of the Council of Trent to serve as precedents for a mitigated application of the penalty of deposition, subsequent legislators limited the infliction of the penalty to those cases wherein the heinous nature of the crime, the criminal's deliberate malintent, or some peculiar aggravating circumstances lent an added malice to the crime perpetrated. Such cases were reflected in voluntary and premeditated murder, in violent rape or adultery, in sacrilegious theft of precious articles, in notorious fornication repeated after warnings, and in public simony.[128] Lending added support to such a lenient application of the law at the close of the last century was the generally recognized legal axiom that no penalty should be imposed for the transgression of a law unless that penalty had been expressly stated in the law (*nulla poena sine lege.*)[129] Because of the general acceptance which this principle found in ecclesiastical courts, one does not find it difficult to concur with Wernz (1842-1914) in his statement that an official codification of the delicts punishable by deposition was greatly to be desired.[130] Such an authentic enumeration of all the crimes upon the commission of which a cleric would be subject to deposition was forthcoming in the penal legislation of the Church, but it was only with the appearance of the Code of Canon Law.

In regard to those crimes which the law of the decretals had punished with degradation, much the same legislation prevailed

[126] Sess. XXV, *de ref.*, c. 14.

[127] Sess. XXII, *Decretum de observandis et evitandis in celebratione Missae.*

[128] Cf. Schmalzgrueber, *Ius Ecclesiasticum Universum,* lib. V, tit. 37, n. 136; Reiffenstuel, *Ius Canonicum Universum,* lib. V, tit. 37, n. 30.

[129] Cf. Wernz, *Ius Decretalium,* VI, n. 123.

[130] *Ius Decretalium, loc. cit.*

during the four centuries now under discussion. Thus degradation was confirmed by Pope Paul IV as a penalty in punishment of heresy, apostasy, and schism.[131] The falsification of papal letters also continued to be punished with the same penalty, but now the penalty was extended to include also all accomplices in the crime as well as the forgers themselves.[132] Similarly punished were grave contumely, calumny, or conspiracy against one's bishop when such delicts were coupled with incorrigibility.[133] Finally, as was true also in the era governed by the law of the decretals, certain other grave crimes, though not explicitly calling for degradation as their punishment, were in fact so punished when milder penalties did not suffice for the correcting of a contumacious, delinquent cleric.

In addition, however, to these examples, wherewith the popes of this period confirmed their predecessors' legislation, other penal laws can be adduced which show the extension of the number of crimes to which the penalty of degradation became applicable. These examples are of two general classes: some show the substitution of degradation for deposition as the punishment for certain classes of crime; others give evidence of entirely new crimes punished with degradation, or at least of crimes regarding which the penalty of degradation was made explicit, though it had theretofore been merely implicit in the general classification of "other more heinous crimes." Examples of crimes regarding which degradation supplanted deposition as their penalty were the cases that involved clerics found guilt of sodomy;[134] the cases of clerics who were guilty of procuring an abortion;[135] the cases wherein a cleric below the order of the priesthood presumed to offer the

---

[131] Const. *Cum ex apostolatus,* 15 febr. 1559, § 2—*Fontes,* n. 94.

[132] Const. *In supremo iustitiae,* 8 apr. 1563 of Pope Innocent X—*Fontes,* n. 234.

[133] Cf. Fagnanus, *Commentaria,* lib. II, tit. 1, cap. 10, n. 71.

[134] Cf. Pope St. Pius V in his const. *Cum primum,* 1 apr. 1566, § 11—*Fontes,* n. 111; const. *Horrendum,* 30 aug. 1568—Fontes, n. 128.

[135] Cf. Pope Sixtus V in his const. *Effraenatum,* 29 oct. 1588, § 4—*Fontes,* n. 165. Three years later this penalty was restricted by Pope Gregory XIV to the punishment of clerics who procured the abortion of an animated fetus (const. *Sedes Apostolica,* 31 maii 1591—*Fontes,* n. 173).

Holy Sacrifice of the Mass or to hear sacramental confessions;[136] and the cases wherein clerics were personally guilty of murder, an extension and augmentation by later canonists of the penalty of deposition as decreed by Pope Innocent IV in the I General Council of Lyons (1245) for any cleric who hired assassins to commit murder for him.[137]

Examples of some of the more atrocious crimes which became specific objects for the penalty of degradation in this period, though previously they had been its object only in so far as they were members of a general class of delicts punishable with degradation, can be drawn both from the universal and from the particular penal law. In Spain, as an example of particular penal law, priests who had been found guilty of solicitation in confession were to be punished with degradation. This penalty was sanctioned in a letter of Pope Pius IV (1560-1565) to the Archbishop of Seville.[138] This penal law was extended to the universal Church and clarified as to its content by Pope Gregory XV (1621-1623).[139] Again, in the following century it was confirmed and further clarified by Pope Benedict XIV.[140] An example of universal legislation that enacted degradation as the penalty for a crime not earlier specifically included in that penalty's ambit was reflected in the case of sacrilegious theft of the Blessed Sacrament. In 1677, Pope Innocent XI (1676-1689) had decreed that such an outrage, even though it were a first offense, was to be punished in the ecclesiastical and secular courts alike, unless it were patent that the thief harbored no evil purpose. No specific mention of clerics was made.[141] Thirteen years later, however, clerical profaners of the Blessed Sacrament were specifically men-

[136] Cf. Pope Clement VIII in his const. *Etsi alias,* 1 dec. 1601—*Fontes,* n. 188; renewed and clarified by Pope Urban VIII (const. *Apostolatus officium,* 23 mart. 1628—*Fontes,* n. 207) and by Pope Benedict XIV (const. *Sacerdos in aeternum,* 20 apr. 1744—*Fontes,* n. 314).

[137] Cf. Fagnanus, *Commentaria,* lib. II, tit. 1, cap. 10, n. 72; lib. V, tit. 39, cap. 45, n. 19. For the relevant text of the Council of Lyons, cf. c. 1, *de homicidio,* V, 4, in VI°.

[138] Ep. *Cum sicut nuper,* 16 apr. 1561—*Fontes,* n. 102.

[139] Const. *Universi,* 30 aug. 1622—*Fontes,* n. 201.

[140] Const. *Sacramentum Poenitentiae,* 1 iun. 1741—CIC, Documentum V.

[141] Const. *Ad Nostri Apostolatus,* 12 mart. 1677—*Fontes,* n. 250.

tioned as subject to the secular courts and penalties, with the provision of a prior degradation.[142]

In addition to the still extant laws that called for degradation in punishment of the earlier specified crimes, to the laws that determined the same penalty for the more recently specified crimes, and to the laws whereby the penalty of deposition was supplanted by that of degradation, there likewise prevailed the law of Pope Celestine III, which had required degradation in punishment of continued incorrigibility, namely after deposition and further penalties had been inflicted in vain.[143]

This last mentioned law, however, became the subject of two controversies in the period now under discussion. One dispute arose concerning the postulated necessity of actually inflicting real degradation on a deposed and incorrigible cleric in order to effect the deprivation of his clerical privileges. Another, granted indeed the necessity of actually inflicting real degradation in order to effect a deprivation of the clerical privileges, concerned itself with the necessity of a previous observance of the various penal procedures which in a sense served to determine the element of incorrigibility, in accord with the legislative demand of Pope Celestine, before the infliction of real degradation could be rightfully undertaken. A brief summary of these two discussions is the subject-matter of the following sections.

Section 3. Controversy on the Necessity of Real Degradation for Effecting the Loss of the Clerical Privileges

From the history presented in the preceding article it will be remembered that Pope Celestine III at the close of the twelfth century had decreed that, if a cleric who had been deposed for theft, perjury, or homicide, remained incorrigible even after deposition, he was to be excommunicated. Then, if his contumacy still endured, he was to be subjected to anathemas employed against him. Finally, if he still persisted in his obduracy, he was

---

[142] Const. of Pope Alexander VIII, *Cum alias,* 22 dec. 1690—*Fontes,* n. 255; confirmed by Pope Benedict XIV in his const. *Ab augustissimo,* 5 mart. 1744—*Fontes,* n. 340.

[143] C. 10, X, *de iudiciis,* II, 1.

to be seized and punished by the secular court.[144] In virtue of this decree, incorrigibility after deposition was held by many reputable commentators on the law of the Decretals (notably Ioannes Andreae (+1348) and Panormitanus (+1453) in the period governed by that body of law) as *ipso facto* effecting a deprivation of the clerical privileges, apart from all necessary infliction of real degradation.[145] Even after the Council of Trent many authors continued to adhere to this opinion as advanced by Ioannes Andreae and Panormitanus in the preceding era. As a matter of fact, it was considered to be the opinion of almost all who treated the subject.[146] Barbosa (1589-1649) gave as his reason for upholding this opinion that there was an assumed degradation derived from the law itself.[147] Similarly, Fagnanus (1598-1678), though styling the opposite opinion the more secure one, nevertheless propounded the same view as Barbosa.[148] Reiffenstuel (1642-1703) called attention to the statement of Fagnanus regarding which opinion was the more secure one, but, like Fagnanus, also maintained that no real degradation was necessary.[149]

Notwithstanding the extrinsic weight of authority which such revered names lent to the probability of this opinion, the opinion gradually lost favor with the post-Tridentine canonists. In the eighteenth century such famous names in canon law as Van Espen (1646-1728),[150] Schmalzgrueber (1663-1735)[151] and Bene-

---

[144] C. 10, X, *de iudiciis,* II, 1.

[145] Cf. Ioannes Andreae, *In Quinque Decretalium Libros Novella Commentaria* (4 vols., Venetiis, 1581), lib. II, tit. 1, *de iudiciis,* c. 10, n. 11 hereafter cited as *Novella Commentaria*); Panormitanus (Nicolaus de Tudeschis), *Commentaria in Quinque Libros Decretalium* (5 vols. in 7, Venetiis, 1588), lib. II, tit. 1, *de iudiciis,* c. 10, n. 28 (hereafter cited as *Commentaria*).

[146] De Grassis, *Tractatus de Effectibus Clericatus* (Venetiis, 1674), Effectus I, n. 797.

[147] *Collectanea,* lib. II, tit. 1, c. 10, n. 9.

[148] *Commentaria,* lib. II, tit. 1, c. 10, nn. 25, 26.

[149] *Ius Canonicum Universum,* lib. II, tit. 2, n. 255.

[150] *Ius Ecclesiasticum Universum* (5 vols. in 2, Coloniae Agrippinae, 1729), Pars III, tit. 2, n. 46.

[151] *Ius Ecclesiasticum Universum,* lib. V, tit. 37, n. 151.

dict XIV (1740-1758)[152] gave the weight of their authority to the opposite opinion, maintaining the necessity of real degradation as a prerequisite for depriving deposed and incorrigible clerics of their clerical privileges. By the following century the opinion of these latter canonists was by far the more common one; in fact it was the one generally held.[153] Consequently, one may infer that perpetual deprivation of the clerical garb (the chief effect of which is deprivation of the clerical privileges) was held by these more recent canonists to be a concomitant part of real or actual degradation alone.

Section 4. Controversy on the Determination of Incorrigibility

Concerning the same decree of Pope Celestine, another dispute was raised in this period. It referred to the question of how incorrigibility on the part of a deposed and contumacious cleric was to be determined. Some authors maintained that it was not necessary to observe the gradation of penal procedures in accordance with which the incorrigibility was to be determined by the decree of Pope Celestine. In their opinion, degradation could be inflicted by the competent authority forthwith, once the deposed cleric had committed a grave crime.[154]

Others, however, with more consistency, propounded the theory that actual degradation could be inflicted on a deposed cleric only after the other remedies provided by Pope Celestine had failed to break down his contumacy, or only if the cleric had been guilty of a delict explicitly punished in law with this gravest of the vindicative penalties.[155] Only the latter viewpoint succeeded in safeguarding the privileged forum for clerics and ecclesiastical liberty in general. Moreover, it was more in harmony with the doctrine of the decretalists.[156]

---

[152] *De synodo dioecesana,* lib. IX, cap. 6, n. 3.

[153] Cf., e.g., Santi-Leitner, *Praelectiones Iuris Canonici* (4. ed., 5 vols. in 4, Ratisbonae, 1903-1905), II, n. 33; Lega, *De Delictis et Poenis,* n. 210; Devoti, *Institutiones,* tit. IV, 21, n. 2.

[154] Cf. the list of authors cited by Schmalzgrueber, *Ius Ecclesiasticum Universum,* lib. V, tit. 37, n. 152.

[155] Cf. Schmalzgrueber, *ibid.,* n. 153.

[156] Fagnanus, *Commentaria,* lib. II, tit. 1, cap. 10, nn. 26-68.

The basic objection to the former opinion was this: the norm which it proposed for the infliction of real degradation was derived not from ecclesiastical legislation on the matter, as one would rightly expect, but rather from civil laws. The proponents of this opinion wanted degradation to be inflicted by the Church law wherever the crime perpetrated was punishable by death in the civil law.[157] Pope Benedict XIV, however, was careful to point out that there would have been no reason for ecclesiastical legislation to specify certain crimes as punishable with degradation if any and all serious delicts could have been thus punished. At the same time he affirmed that, outside of the delicts specifically punished in law with degradation, the opinion which held to the necessity of observing his predecessor's gradation of penal procedures and imposed penalties for determining incorrigibility was the opinion commonly espoused and the one to be followed in practice by the bishops throughout the world.[158] Accordingly, Pope Celestine's rules continued to be followed in their pristine order up to the enactment of the Code of Canon Law.[159]

One may conclude, therefore, with a good deal of probability that deprivation of the clerical garb in this period was not inflicted on a deposed cleric until he was actually punished with the penalty of real degradation. This latter penalty, in turn, could follow only after a cleric's incorrigibility had been determined in line with the demands inherent in the decree of Pope Celestine. Actual degradation was to remain the only way in which a cleric could be deprived of his peculiar garb up until the appearance of the Code of Canon Law with the newly enacted penalty of deprivation of the clerical garb as listed therein.[160]

---

[157] Fagnanus, *loc. cit.*

[158] *De synodo dioecesana,* lib. IX, cap. 6, nn. 10, 11.

[159] Cf. Wernz, *Ius Decretalium,* VI, n. 136.

[160] Cf. Wernz-Vidal, *Ius Canonicum,* VII, n. 352, fn. 147: "Cum iure praecedenti citra degradationem realem clerico in sacris privilegia clericalia auferri non poterant, ita non poterant facultate gestandi habitum clericalem spoliari et ad statum laicalem redigi. . . ."

PART TWO

Canonical Commentary

CHAPTER III

NATURE AND EFFECTS OF THE PENALTY OF DEPRIVATION OF THE CLERICAL GARB

ARTICLE 1. NATURE OF THE PENALTY

The Code defines an ecclesiastical penalty in general as the privation of some good inflicted by legitimate ecclesiastical authority for the twofold purpose of correcting the delinquent and punishing the delict.[1] The specific nature of deprivation of the clerical garb, therefore (as the specific nature of any other ecclesiastical penalty), can be determined through an examination of what species of good is taken away thereby and through a determination of which of the two purposes is predominant in the penalty's infliction. From a canonical viewpoint, the goods which a penalty can deprive one of are either temporal (natural), such as life, liberty, honor, material possessions, or spiritual (supernatural), such as the rights proper to the lay, clerical, or religious states in the Church.[2] Deprivation of the clerical garb, therefore, is a spiritual penalty, since it deprives the delinquent of rights proper to the clerical state. The foregoing suffices for the classification of deprivation of the clerical garb according to the good deprived; it now remains to determine the nature of this penalty from the purpose which moves the Church to inflict it.

When the purpose of correcting the delinquent is predominant in a penalty's infliction, the penalty is styled a medicinal penalty or a censure,[3] and must be remitted by way of absolution when it has achieved its purpose, viz., when the delinquent has amended his ways by receding from his contumacy.[4] If, on the other hand,

[1] Canon 2215.

[2] Cf. Roberti, *De Delictis et Poenis* (Vol. I, pars I, *De Delictis in Genere*, 2. ed. rev.; Vol. I, pars II, *De Poenis in Genere. De Censuris in Genere et in Specie*, 2. ed., Romae: apud Custodiam Librariam Pontificii Instituti Utriusque Iuris, 1944), Vol. I, pars II, p. 255, n. 230 (hereafter cited as *De Delictis in Genere* and *De Poenis in Genere* respectively).

[3] Canon 2241.

[4] Canon 2248, § 2.

the vindication of the disrupted social order by the punishment of the delict is the main purpose which the Church has in mind when inflicting a penalty, then the penalty is called vindicative.[5] As such it must be fully expiated. If it be remitted before total expiation is made, this result can ensue only as a favor in the form of a dispensation from its further observance granted the culprit by the legitimate superior.[6] Deprivation of the clerical garb (whether for a time or *in perpetuum*) is of this latter category. It is a spiritual vindicative penalty inflicted solely on clerics, as is evident from its position in the Code.[7] As such, it is meant primarily as a punishment for the delict perpetrated, and need not be remitted until the delict has been fully expiated. If it should be remitted beforehand, the dispensation from its full observance is purely a matter of favor and can in no way be demanded by the cleric so punished.

In addition to these divisions into spiritual and temporal, medicinal and vindicative, the Code also distinguishes between *latae sententiae* and *ferendae sententiae* penalties. The former are incurred automatically upon violation of the law or precept to which they are attached. Usually there will be some phrase such as *ipso iure, eo ipso, ipso facto,* etc., which will clearly show that the penalty is incurred automatically.[8] *Ferendae sententiae penalties,* on the other hand, are never incurred except through the intervention of a judge or a superior.[9] Usually such penalties will be expressed in words referring to the future (e.g., *ab Ordinario puniatur, deponatur,* etc.). All penalties are to be considered as *ferendae sententiae* unless the contrary is clearly evident.[10] Thus deprivation of the clerical garb, in addition to being a spiritual vindicative penalty, is also a *ferendae sententiae* penalty, as is evident from the verb phrases used in the two canons which refer to this penalty, namely, *"potest interim privari"* of canon 2300 and *"potest . . . perpetuo privare"* of canon 2304, § 1.

[5] Canon 2286.

[6] Canon 2289; cf. Ayrinhac, *Penal Legislation,* p. 116.

[7] Canon 2298, 9°, 11°, under Lib. V, Tit. IX, Cap. II, *De peculiaribus clericorum poenis vindicativis.*

[8] Canon 2217, § 1, 2° and § 2.

[9] Canon 2217, § 1, 2°.

[10] Canon 2217, § 2; cf. Ayrinhac, *Penal Legislation,* p. 28.

Another distinction which the Code makes in its classification of penalties is the division into penalties incurred *a iure* and *ab homine*. Penalties are said to be incurred *a iure* when, whether *latae* or *ferendae sententiae,* they are determined and enacted by law, universal or particular, or by a general precept.[11] They are said to be incurred *ab homine* when, even though prescribed by law, they are inflicted by way of a particular precept of the superior or by way of a condemnatory sentence of the judge. Hence *ferendae sententiae* penalties, even though determined by law or general precept, will in all practical cases stand as penalties deriving *ab homine.* After infliction they derive in reality *a iure et ab homine,* but are considered simply as deriving *ab homine.*[12] Deprivation of the garb accordingly, since it is a *ferendae sententiae* penalty, will at the same time always be regarded as deriving *ab homine* in any practical case which arises.

One other division remains. Penalties are said to be determined or undetermined according to whether or not a particular law or precept carries with it a specified penalty for its violation, or commits to the prudent decision of the superior or judge the determination of whatever penalty, if any, is to be inflicted.[13] In this respect, deprivation of the clerical garb (temporary or perpetual) may be considered an undetermined penalty. Nowhere in the Code will one find deprivation of the garb listed as the specific penalty for a specific crime committed by a cleric. Rather, its infliction is left to the prudent judgment of the cleric's superior or his delegate, who will inflict it only when all the circumstances warranting its infliction are present in a particular case. Thus the violation of any number of clerical obligations may yield a sufficient cause for temporarily depriving an offending cleric of his distinctive garb, provided scandal is given by the violation, which scandal can be removed in no other way than by the infliction of a temporary deprivation of the offender's garb, since the culprit refuses to heed all admonitions to desist from his scandalous conduct. The same holds true with respect to a perpetual deprivation of the garb. Its infliction too is left to the

[11] Canon 2217, § 1, 3°; cf. Ayrinhac, *loc. cit.*
[12] Canon 2277, § 1, 3°.
[13] Canon 2217, § 1, 1°.

prudent discretion of the superior or his delegate. He must determine whether or not circumstances in a given case warrant its infliction. Those circumstances must indicate incorrigibility after deposition, but they are undetermined, since they may be acts either of commission (in so far as the culprit continues to give scandal) or of omission (in so far as the delinquent fails to amend), as Findlay so well points out.[14] All these distinctions will assume importance when the infliction and remission of deprivation of the clerical garb are taken into consideration in subsequent chapters of this dissertation. In addition to these general notions concerning the nature of the penalty in question, there are a few specific notions which will become apparent from a perusal of the penalty's effects in the following article.

ARTICLE 2. EFFECTS OF THE PENALTY

Section 1. Effect on Acts of Orders and Jurisdiction

Concerning the effect of a deprivation of the clerical garb on acts of orders and acts of jurisdiction placed by the defrocked cleric, it will be necessary to treat temporary and perpetual deprivation separately. As far as temporary deprivation of the clerical garb is concerned, one can say without hesitation that this penalty certainly renders all such acts illicit, but by no means invalid. All authors are in agreement on this point.[15] With regard to the effect which *perpetual* deprivation of the clerical garb has

---

[14] Cf. *Deposition and Degradation,* p. 177.

[15] Cf. canon 2300: ". . . privatio, dum perdurat, secumfert prohibitionem exercendi ministeria quaevis ecclesiastica . . ."; Coronata, *Institutiones Iuris Canonici* (5 vols., Romae: Marietti; Vol. IV, 3. ed., 1947), p. 272, n. 1832: "Nomine ministeriorum ecclesiasticorum quaelibet ordinis aut iurisdictionis potestas venit. . . . Prohibitio per se non dicit invaliditatem actorum contra prohibitionem positorum" (hereafter cited as *Institutiones*); Augustine, *Commentary,* VIII, 259: "The clergyman thus punished is not allowed to perform any act of his ecclesiastical ministry. The text does not declare the invalidity of such acts, e.g., of jurisdiction exercised in the confessional, or assistance at marriage, . . . ; therefore, the least is to be taken"; Berutti, *Institutiones Iuris Canonici,* Vol. VI, *De Delictis et Poenis* (Taurini-Romae: Marietti, 1938), p. 232, n. 89, 9° (hereafter cited as *De Delictis et Poenis*): "Clericus qui hac poena tenetur, nullum actum potestatis sive ordinis sive iurisdictionis *licite* ponere potest." Italics are the present writer's.

on such acts, however, a distinction must be made. Any act of jurisdiction placed by a perpetually defrocked cleric is not only illicit, but also invalid; acts of orders placed by such clerics are likewise illicit, but nonetheless valid.[16] Berutti is the only author whom the present writer has found who explicitly states this fact. The truth of the statement is obvious, however, when one recalls that acts of orders and acts of jurisdiction placed by a *deposed* cleric are subject to the same distinction; the former being valid but illicit, the latter being both illicit and invalid.[17] Since deposition is always postulated as a prerequisite to the infliction of perpetual deprivation of the clerical garb (as will be shown in a succeeding chapter), it is evident that acts of jurisdiction placed by a perpetually defrocked cleric will likewise be invalid. The only doubt that might arise would concern itself with the question of whether or not acts of orders placed by a perpetually defrocked cleric remain merely illicit and not invalid (as they remain when placed by deposed clerics who have not had their deposition augmented by perpetual deprivation). The doubt disappears when one considers that acts of orders placed even by a degraded cleric (and degradation is the most severe of the vindicative penalties peculiar to clerics) remain valid though they likewise be illicit.[18] *A fortiori,* the same must be true with reference to a perpetual deprivation of the garb, since this penalty is included in degradation as a constituent element.[19] The reason of course why all acts of orders remain valid (no matter how severely punished the cleric placing such actions be) is the fact that sacred ordination once validly received is never invalidated.[20] The power inherent in the orders received is therefore never lost, and consequently actions placed in virtue of that power are always valid, though they may be illicit because of a penalty incurred by the cleric placing them. In regard to the power of orders, then, deprivation of the clerical garb (whether for a time or *in perpetuum*) does not take away

[16] Cf. Berutti, *op. cit.*, p. 235.

[17] Cf. Coronata, *Institutiones*, IV, p. 274, n. 1834.

[18] Cf. Ayrinhac, *Penal Legislation*, p. 130, n. 172.

[19] Canon 2305, § 1.

[20] Canon 211, § 1.

the power itself, but only renders its use unlawful. A defrocked cleric would sin gravely by exercising his orders; nevertheless he would act validly. The only time that such a cleric would act invalidly would be in the supposition that he had been *perpetually* deprived of his garb and attempted to place an action which simultaneously required not only the power of orders but also that of jurisdiction (e.g., the hearing of confessions). Here it might help to mention, however, that a defrocked priest can in one instance, in virtue of an exception granted by the law itself, exercise his power to administer the sacrament of penance licitly as well as validly. That one instance is the case wherein such a priest is called upon to hear the confession of one of the faithful *in periculo mortis.* In that case the defrocked priest can absolve both validly and licitly from all sins and censures, no matter in what way they be reserved or to what extent they be notorious. This he can do even if a priest approved for the hearing of confessions be also present.[21] If no other priest were available, he could also administer to the dying penitent the sacraments of Extreme Unction and Holy Viaticum.[22] Outside of this one exceptional case, any cleric in major orders who has been deprived of his garb would incur an irregularity *ex delicto* if he exercised any act of orders the performance of which has been forbidden him in virtue of this penalty.[23] This irregularity would be incurred, however, only if the defrocked cleric *solemnly* placed the proscribed

---

[21] Canon 882: "In periculo mortis omnes sacerdotes, licet ad confessiones non approbati, valide et licite absolvunt quoslibet poenitentes a quibusvis peccatis aut censuris, quantumvis reservatis et notoriis, etiamsi praesens sit sacerdos approbatus, salvo praescripto can. 884, 2252"; cf. Cappello, *Tractatus Canonico Moralis de Sacramentis,* Vol. II, *De Poenitentia* (5. ed., Taurinorum Augustae: Marietti, 1943), pp. 366-sqq., n. 395; Kelly, *Jurisdiction of the Confessor According to the Code of Canon Law* (New York: Benziger Bros., 1929), pp. 92-93.

[22] Cf. Cappello, *op. cit.,* Vol. I, *De Sacramentis in genere, de Baptismo, Confirmatione, et Eucharistia* (5. ed., *ibidem,* 1945), p. 69, n. 78; canon 2261, § 3.

[23] Canon 985, 7°: "Sunt irregulares ex delicto: . . . Qui actum ordinis, clericis in ordine sacro constitutis reservatum, ponunt, vel eo ordine carentes, vel ab eius exercitio poena canonica sive personali, medicinali aut vindicativa, sive locali prohibiti."

act.[24] At the same time he would have to be guilty of an external grave sin.[25]

It might also be pointed out here that the defrocked cleric (even though he be forbidden to place acts of orders) could lawfully exercise certain functions of *minor* orders which laymen are permitted to exercise according to the practice of the Church. Such functions as the serving of Mass and acting as a sexton are in practice committed to laymen. Evidently these functions are not to be considered then as exclusively proper to the clerical state. Accordingly, canonists state that a suspended cleric can licitly perform these functions as a layman.[26] There seems to be no reason why the same should not hold true with regard to defrocked clerics, even though deprivation of the clerical garb is distinct from and more severe than suspension. In accordance with the axiom, "In poenis benignior est interpretatio facienda,"[27] the restriction placed on the defrocked cleric's liberty must be constrained to those acts of orders which are exclusively proper to the clerical state and should not be extended to include those acts which in practice can be and are performed by laymen.

What might be noted here also is that clerics who have been punished with deprivation of their garb are in no wise prevented from administering the sacrament of baptism *privately* (as indeed any layman is empowered to do) when the circumstances calling for such a course of action are present in a particular case.[28] In such cases, however, the defrocked cleric may perform lawfully

---

[24] Cf. Vermeersch-Creusen, *Epitome Iuris Canonici* (3 vols., Mechliniae-Romae: Dessain, 1934-1937. Vol. I, 6. ed., 1937; Vol. II, 5. ed., 1934; Vol. III, 5. ed., 1936), II, p. 176, n. 257 (hereafter cited as *Epitome*).

[25] Canon 986.

[26] Cf. Vermeersch-Creusen, *Epitome*, III, p. 287, n. 482; Coronata, *Institutiones*, I (3. ed., 1947), p. 196, n. 181; Roberti, *De Poenis in Genere*, p. 487, n. 381; p. 491, n. 382; Cocchi, *Commentarium in Codicem Iuris Canonici ad Usum Scholarum* (8 vols., Taurinorum Augustae: Marietti; Vol. I, 5. ed., 1938; Vol. II, 4. ed., 1937; Vol. III, 3. ed., 1931; Vol. IV, 3. ed., 1932; Vol. V, 3. ed., 1932; Vol. VI, 3. ed., 1933; Vol. VII, 3. ed., 1940; Vol. VIII, 4. ed., 1938), VIII, p. 175, n. 103 (hereafter cited as *Commentarium*).

[27] Canon 2219, § 1.

[28] Canon 743, § 1.

only those rites which are necessary for the valid administration of the sacrament; he may in no way perform those ceremonies which are reserved to priests and deacons in the solemn administration of the same sacrament.[29]

Before this section be brought to a close, a few remarks explanatory of the diverse effects which temporary and perpetual deprivation have on acts of jurisdiction are in order. It has already been said that acts of jurisdiction placed by a cleric temporarily bereft of his ecclesiastical garb are illicit; these same acts when placed by a cleric perpetually deprived of his garb are invalid. Why the difference? The authors for the most part give no reason. The answer, however, is manifest. The reason is this: jurisdiction which is ordinary is in such a manner attached by law to an ecclesiastical office that the cleric who acquires the office automatically acquires the jurisdiction connected with it.[30] Vice versa, he loses this jurisdiction[31] when he is deprived of the office.[32] As will be shown in a subsequent section of this article, the cleric temporarily deprived of his garb does not lose his office; the cleric perpetually deprived of his garb has already lost his by the fact that he has been deposed. As far as ordinary jurisdiction goes, therefore, the former still has the power, though he is forbidden to use it; the latter has already lost all such power along with the office which entitled him to it even before he has been perpetually deprived of his right to wear the clerical garb. Thus the temporarily defrocked cleric's acts of jurisdiction will be illicit only; the perpetually defrocked cleric's acts of jurisdiction will be not only unlawful, but also invalid. The same holds true with regard to the delegated jurisdiction which a cleric may hold. Delegated jurisdiction is always committed to a person who accordingly is to act with authority in the Church.[33] To act on such a commission is prohibited when a cleric is temporarily deprived of his right to wear the garb, but action taken in the face of such a prohibition is considered

[29] Canon 759, § 1; cf. Roberti, *De Poenis in Genere,* p. 491, n. 382.
[30] Canon 197, § 1.
[31] Canons 208; 873, § 3.
[32] Canon 183, § 1.
[33] Canon 197, § 1.

valid though illicit.[34] Such a commission, on the other hand, has actually been lost by a cleric who is perpetually deprived of his garb. The reason lies in the fact that he has been deposed, for deposition deprives a cleric not only of all offices in the strict sense,[35] but also of any office, function, or charge committed only to clerics under the ordinary law of the Church.[36] For a perpetually defrocked cleric, therefore, to act in view of jurisdiction which was delegated to him prior to his deposition would be invalid. One may likewise note here that the same distinction will hold true with reference to acts of orders placed by defrocked clerics, if they were empowered to place these acts of orders not by any order which they themselves have received, but in virtue of delegation either by law or indult. Thus a priest who has the faculty to confirm would do so illicitly if he is temporarily deprived of his right to wear the clerical garb, and invalidly if he is perpetually shorn of it.[37]

Section 2. Effect on Clerical Obligations

Neither of the two canons (2300 and 2304) which specifically treat of deprivation of the clerical garb makes any explicit reference to the effect which this penalty has on the defrocked cleric's obligations. Nor do the authors for the most part have anything to say on the particular point in question. If one looks to their commentary, however, on the effect which the penalties of deposition and degradation (to which penalties deprivation of the garb is so closely allied) have on these same obligations, much light will be shed on the subject. Because of the fact that in practice this penalty will usually be inflicted only on clerics in major orders,[38] this discussion will be confined to the effect which the penalty in question has on the chief obligations of a cleric

[34] Cf. fn. 15 *supra*.

[35] Canon 145, § 1.

[36] Canon 2303, § 1; cf. Findlay, *Deposition and Degradation*, p. 150.

[37] Cf. canon 782, §§ 2 and 3, Maroto, *Institutiones Iuris Canonici ad Normam Novi Codicis*, 2 vols., Vol. I, *Tractatus Fundamentales* (3. ed., Romae: apud Commentarium pro Religiosis, 1921), p. 878, n. 733; Wernz, *Ius Decretalium*, II, p. 333, n. 231.

[38] Cf. pp. 80-90.

in major orders, viz., to the effect which deprivation of the clerical garb has on the obligations of celibacy and the daily recitation of the Divine Office.[39]

With reference to *temporary* deprivation of the garb, it can be stated with moral certainty that the major cleric temporarily bereft of his distinctive garb remains bound by these two obligations. The writer has found only one author who explicitly states this.[40] There seems to be no reasonable cause, however, for doubting this statement, since it is unanimously held that a cleric, even when there has been inflicted upon him the penalty of deposition (which is a more severe penalty than temporary deprivation of the garb in so far as it is *per se* perpetual), remains so bound.[41] With reference to the effect which *perpetual* deprivation of the garb has on these two obligations of the major cleric so punished, a separate treatment for each obligation is called for. As far as the obligation of celibacy is concerned, it can be stated with moral certainty that the obligation remains. This is evident from the

[39] Canons 132 and 135.

[40] Cf. Pellé, *Le Droit Pénal de L'Église* (Paris: P. Lethielleux, 1939), p. 179: "il reste lié par les obligations de son ordre (célibat, bréviaire)."

[41] Cf., e.g., canon 2303, § 1: "Depositio, firmis obligationibus e suscepto ordine exortis . . ."; Augustine, *Commentary,* VIII, 260; Wernz-Vidal, *Ius Canonicum,* VII, p. 375, n. 352; Coronata, *Institutiones,* IV, p. 275, n. 1836; Ayrinhac, *Penal Legislation,* p. 128, n. 168; Berutti, *De Delictis et Poenis,* p. 233, n. 90, II; Prümmer, *Manuale Iuris Canonici* (4. et 5. ed., Friburgi Brisgoviae: Herder and Co., 1927), p. 669, q. 579; Blat, *Commentarium Textus Codicis Iuris Canonici* (5 vols. in 7, Romae: Collegio "Angelico"; Vol. I, 1921; Vol. II, pars I, 2. ed., 1921; Vol. II, partes II et III, 3. ed., 1938; Vol. III, pars I, 2. ed., 1924; Vol. III, partes II-VI, 2. ed., 1934; Vol. IV, 1927; Vol. V, 1924), V, p. 185, n. 136 (hereafter cited as *Commentarium*); Vermeersch-Creusen, *Epitome,* III, p. 300, n. 498; Cocchi, *Commentarium,* VIII, p. 200, n. 118; Sipos, *Enchiridion Iuris Canonici* (Pécs: Ex Typographis "Haladás R. T.," 1926), § 240, p. 947 (hereafter cited as *Enchiridion*); Chelodi, *Ius Poenale,* p. 69, n. 52; Sole, *Praelectiones in Lib. V Codicis Iuris Canonici, De Delictis et Poenis* (Romae: Pustet, 1920), p. 205, n. 290 (hereafter cited as *De Delictis et Poenis*); Eichmann, *Das Strafrecht des Codex Iuris Canonici* (Paderborn: Ferdinand Schöningh, 1920), pp. 119-120 (hereafter cited as *Das Strafrecht*); Naz, *Traité de Droit Canonique* (5 books in 4 toms., Paris: Letouzey et Ané, 1947-1948), Tom. IV, lib. 5, *Des Délits et des Peines* (ed. by E. Jombart), p. 691, n. 1116 (hereafter cited as Jombart, *Des Délits de des Peines*).

fact that even a degraded cleric remains so bound.[42] As to the effect of perpetual deprivation on the major cleric's obligation of daily reciting the Divine Office, however, there appears to be some room for doubt. The doubt arises from a dispute among the authors as to whether or not a *degraded* cleric remains so bound. It has already been pointed out that a deposed cleric is still obliged to the daily recitation of his Divine Office, and, as will be pointed out in a subsequent chapter of this dissertation, a cleric must be first deposed before he can be perpetually deprived of his right to wear the garb. Accordingly, it seems that the perpetually defrocked cleric is still bound by this obligation unless perpetual deprivation itself released him. Such a possibility might be considered when one realizes that there are some authors who aver that a degraded cleric is no longer bound to the recitation of his breviary.[43] Others there are who assert that the obligation is at least doubtful.[44] Still others maintain that the obligation remains in force.[45] If it could be proved that a degraded cleric is no longer bound by the obligation of reciting his Divine Office, then one might still inquire whether the obligation had ceased by reason of degradation that has been inflicted, or by reason of perpetual deprivation which had been inflicted subsequent to the deposition but antecedent to the degradation. A brief examination of the argument adduced by the exponents of the opinion that a degraded

---

[42] Cf. canon 213, §§ 1 and 2; cf. also Ayrinhac, *Penal Legislation,* p. 132, n. 175; Augustine, *Commentary,* VIII, 262; Coronata, *Institutiones,* IV, p. 275, n. 1836; Blat, *Commentarium,* V, p. 186, n. 138; Findlay, *Deposition and Degradation,* pp. 212-213; Jombart, *Des Délits et des Peines,* p. 691, n. 1118.

[43] Cf. Augustine, *Commentary,* VIII, 262, fn. 19; Ayrinhac, *Penal Legislation,* p. 132, n. 175; Chelodi, *Ius Poenale,* p. 71, n. 53; Findlay, *Deposition and Degradation,* pp. 213-217.

[44] Cf., e.g., Cocchi, *Commentarium,* VIII, p. 202, n. 119; Vermeersch-Creusen, *Epitome,* III, p. 304, n. 499, 1; Sipos, *Enchiridion,* § 240, p. 948, not. 12; § 34, p. 161, not. 4; De Meester, *Juris Canonici et Juris Canonico-Civilis Compendium* (nova ed., 3 vols. in 4, Brugis: Desclée, 1921-1928), III, pars 2, p. 226, n. 1799 (hereafter cited as *Compendium*); Beste, *Introductio in Codicem* (3. ed., Collegeville, Minnesota: St. John's Abbey Press, 1946), p. 952.

[45] Cf., e.g., Coronata, *Institutiones,* IV, p. 275, n. 1836; Jombart, *Des Délits et des Peines,* p. 691, n. 1118.

cleric is no longer bound (or at least only doubtfully bound) by the recitation of the Office will prove of great help in solving the question. Their argument in brief is this. The law of the Code expressly indicates that clerics in major orders who have been legitimately reduced to the lay state are excepted from the general rule that binds all clerics in major orders to the obligation of daily reciting the canonical hours completely according to their proper and approved liturgical books.[46] Such a legitimate reduction to the lay state, they continue, has occurred in the case of major clerics who have been degraded.[47] Therefore, they conclude, degraded major clerics are no longer bound to the recitation of the Divine Office.

In the opinion of the writer this conclusion seems not without some warrant. It is to be noted, however, that the reason why these authors maintain that a degraded major cleric is released from his obligation of daily reciting the canonical hours is the fact that he has been reduced to the lay state, and reduction to the lay state is a constituent element of the penalty of degradation alone. Accordingly, the apparent doubt with regard to the same effect as resulting from perpetual deprivation of the garb evanesces, since degradation is the only penalty by which a major cleric can be reduced to the lay state.[48] Thus one can see that the opinion which Leitner (1862-1929) advanced at the beginning of this century, namely that perpetual privation of the right to wear the clerical garb of itself probably reduced the cleric to the lay state,

---

[46] Canon 135: "Clerici in maioribus ordinibus constituti, exceptis iis de quibus in can. 213 . . . , tenentur obligatione quotidie horas canonicas integre recitandi secundum proprios et probatos liturgicos libros" and canon 213, § 1: "Omnes qui e clericali statu ad laicalem legitime redacti aut regressi sunt, eo ipso amittunt officia, beneficia, iura ac privilegia clericalia et vetantur in habitu ecclesiastico incedere ac tonsuram deferre."

[47] Canon 211, § 1: "Etsi sacra ordinatio, semel valide recepta, nunquam irrita fiat, clericus tamen maior ad statum laicalem redigitur rescripto Sanctae Sedis, decreto vel sententia ad normam can. 214, demum poena degradationis" and canon 2305, § 1: "Degradatio in se continet depositionem, perpetuam privationem habitus ecclesiastici, et reductionem clerici ad statum laicalem."

[48] Cf. Findlay, *Deposition and Degradation*, pp. 178, 206, 210, 217.

is untenable.[49] Quite the contrary of Leitner's contention obtains. The deposed and perpetually defrocked cleric, sad though his plight be, is nonetheless still a cleric.[50] Consequently, he is still obliged to the daily recitation of his Divine Office. With Berutti (the only author whom the writer has been able to find who explicitly treats the question), therefore, one can conclude that a major cleric who has been perpetually deprived of his distinctive garb still remains bound by his obligations of celibacy and the breviary, just as a major cleric who is deprived of his garb only temporarily remains so bound.[51]

Section 3. Effect on Office

With regard to the effect which deprivation of an offending cleric's garb will have on any office which he may happen to hold, the following might be pointed out. If the penalty in question be inflicted only in its temporary form, i.e., for a set period of time (e.g., six months, one year, etc.) or for some indefinite period (e.g., *ad beneplacitum nostrum*) which is not meant to be perpetual then the office held will not be lost. Canon 2300 makes no explicit mention of this fact, but all authors are in agreement on the point.[52] This does not mean that the clerical officeholder so punished can still perform the acts of jurisdiction which he ordinarily could perform in virtue of the office which he holds. In the first section of this article it has already been pointed out that such acts would be illicit.

The same cannot be said with regard to the effect of perpetual

[49] Cf. *Lehrbuch des katholischen Eherechts* (Paderborn, 1902), p. 256; cf. also Hilling, *Das Personenrecht des Codex Iuris Canonici* (Paderborn: Ferdinand Schöningh, 1924), p. 84, not. 1.

[50] Cf. Chelodi, *Ius Poenale*, 69, n. 52.

[51] Cf. *De Delictis et Poenis*, p. 235, n. 91, II: "Prorsus indubium est quod clericus, hac poena (i.e., perpetual deprivation of the garb) mulctatus, adhuc obstrictus manet obligationibus e suscepto ordine exortis, ad normam praescripti can. 2303, § 1."

[52] Cf., e.g., Augustine, *Commentary*, VIII, 259, where, in the author's commentary on canon 2300, it is stated that "the text does not declare . . . the loss of the respective office; therefore, the least is to be taken"; Coronata, *Institutiones*, IV, p. 272, n. 1832: "Officium tamen hac poena non amittitur"; Eichmann, *Das Strafrecht*, p. 119: "Das Amt selbst entzieht sie nicht."

deprivation of the clerical garb on any office which the cleric so punished may have possessed. Strictly, indeed, neither does perpetual deprivation entail the loss of office, but the reason is that any office which the culprit may have held has already been lost through the infliction of deposition,[63] which is always required as a prerequisite step before perpetual privation of the garb can be inflicted.[64] What has been said concerning the effect of this penalty on the defrocked cleric's office applies with equal force to any benefice, dignity, pension, or assignment which he may hold.

Section 4. Effect on the Defrocked Cleric's Revenue

Canon 2300 does not make any mention of any effect which temporary deprivation of the garb has on the ecclesiastical revenue of the cleric so punished. Neither do the authors have anything to say on the subject. From what has been said in previous sections of this article, however, one can infer that the cleric temporarily deprived of his garb does not inherently suffer any loss of income from the fact that he has been hampered with this penalty. This is evident from the fact that he retains any office, benefice, dignity, or pension, which he may hold, as was pointed out in the previous section. Accordingly, he seems to be entitled to any income which accrues from such an office, benefice, etc. For incidental reasons he may suffer some loss of income by reason of the fact that he needs to employ a substitute in order to fulfill certain duties which are incumbent upon him by reason of the office or benefice which he holds (e.g., the obligation of saying the *"Missa pro populo"* as attaching to a parochial benefice) and which he cannot fulfill in person by reason of the fact that any such action would be illicit, as was pointed out in the first section of this article. Perpetual deprivation of the clerical garb, on the other hand, has a direct and primary effect on the ecclesiastical revenue of the cleric so punished. In the canon which treats of

[63] Cf., e.g., canon 2303, § 1: "Depositio . . . secumfert tum suspensionem ab officio, et inhabilitatem ad quaelibet officia, dignitates, beneficia, pensiones, munera in Ecclesia, tum etiam privationem illorum quae reus habeat, licet eorum titulo fuerit ordinatus." Cf. also Ayrinhac, *Penal Legislation,* p. 128, n. 168; Findlay, *Deposition and Degradation,* pp. 151-152.

[64] Cf. pp. 100-102.

deposition, it is explicitly stated that the deposed cleric loses all offices, benefices, dignities, or pensions which he may have possessed, and becomes incapable of acquiring them in the future.[55] Consequently, the deposed cleric loses all his sources of ecclesiastical revenue since he loses the office, benefice, etc., which entitled him to this revenue. The same canon, however, provides that the ordinary should see to it that such a deposed cleric is given some charitable assistance if he be truly in need lest he be forced to beg with consequent dishonor to the clerical state. Findlay is careful to point out that such charitable aid is provided for by the Code not so much to show concern for the deposed cleric but to safeguard the honor due the clerical state, since a deposed cleric still has the right to go about clad in his distinctive clerical garb, which would bring dishonor on the clerical state if, when so clad, he engaged in secular pursuits or went about as a mendicant.[56] Accordingly, once the deposed cleric has been perpetually deprived of his right to wear the clerical garb because of continued incorrigibility even after deposition, the reason for such a charitable allowance ceases, and the ordinary is no longer compelled to provide such aid. Canon 2304 explicitly states this fact.[57]

Section 5. Effect on Clerical Privileges

Both canons which treat of deprivation of the clerical garb speak of the privation of the clerical privileges as one of the penalty's effects.[58] Accordingly, no matter whether the penalty be inflicted *in perpetuum* or for a time only, it could seem that the clerical privileges would be lost. That such is not the case with regard to the effect which *temporary* deprivation has on these

[55] Canon 2303, § 1; cf. Findlay, *Deposition and Degradation*, pp. 151-156, 167.

[56] Cf. Findlay, *op. cit.*, p. 168.

[57] Canon 2304, § 2: "Haec privatio secumfert privationem privilegiorum clericalium et cessationem praescripti can. 2303, § 2."

[58] Canon 2300: ". . . potest interim privari iure deferendi habitum ecclesiasticum; quae privatio, dum perdurat, secumfert . . . privationem privilegiorum clericalium," and 2304, § 2: "Haec privatio [i.e., perpetua] secumfert privationem privilegiorum clericalium. . . ."

privileges is evident from the fact that the Code qualifies the effects enumerated in canon 2300 with the phrase, *"dum perdurat."* What is evidently meant, therefore, is that temporary deprivation of a cleric's garb results in a penal suspension of his clerical privileges, rather than in an actual loss of them. The truth of this statement is apparent from an earlier canon in the Code which *ex professo* treats of the way in which these clerical privileges can be lost, and from the commentary given by various authors on canon 2300.[59] As to the fact that perpetual deprivation of a cleric's garb, on the other hand, actually does result in a true loss of these same privileges there can be no question, in view of the explicit wording of the canons.[60] Since it has already been pointed out in the historical synopsis what these clerical privileges are (namely, the privileges of the canon, of the forum, of immunity, and of competence), they need not be treated again at this point. What may be stressed, however, is the fact that the phrase, "clerical privileges," as used in canons 2300 and 2304, does not include the prerogative mentioned in canon 118 of the title in the Code which treats of clerical privileges and rights.[61] This is evident from the fact that canon 118 mentions that only clerics are capable of acquiring ecclesiastical power either of orders or of jurisdiction, as well as benefices and ecclesiastical pensions. It has already been pointed out in a preceding section of this

[59] Cf. canon 123: "Memoratis privilegiis clericus renuntiare nequit; sed eadem amittit, si ad statum laicalem reducatur aut privatione perpetua iuris deferendi habitum ecclesiasticum plectatur, ad normam can. 213, § 1, 2304; . . ." Arguing from this canon's silence with regard to temporary deprivation of the clerical garb as contrasted with its explicit mention of *perpetual* deprivation as one of the ways in which the clerical privileges are lost, reputable canonists justifiably assert that temporary deprivation results only in a penal suspension of the privileges, and not in a true loss of them. Cf., e.g., Berutti, *De Delictis et Poenis,* p. 232, n. 89, 9°: "Neque communibus clericorum privilegiis gaudet, de quibus in cc. 119-122, quamvis eadem non proprie amittat"; Blat, *Commentarium,* V, p. 184, n. 133: ". . . privationem in hoc canone idem sonare ac suspensionem eorundem privilegiorum poenalem"; De Meester, *Compendium,* III, pars 2, p. 224, n. 1795, not. 6; Findlay, *Deposition and Degradation,* p. 173; *Diarium Romanae Curiae, Communicatio—AAS,* XIX (1927), 290.

[60] Canons 123 and 2304, § 2.

[61] Lib. II, tit. II, *CIC.*

article that a cleric temporarily deprived of his garb does not lose his power of orders or of jurisdiction, though his use of such power would be illicit. It has also been established that he retains any office which he may have had in the Church. At the same time it was indicated that a cleric perpetually deprived of his distinctive dress acts invalidly (except in the circumstances mentioned) when he places an act of jurisdiction. It was likewise shown that such a cleric does not lose any office, benefice, etc., when he is perpetually deprived of his garb, since all such offices, etc., have already been lost through the infliction of the penalty of deposition which was necessarily prerequisite to the infliction of the penalty in question. Accordingly, the phrase, "clerical privileges," as used in canons 2300 and 2304, must be restricted to the privileges which all clerics in general enjoy as members of the clerical state, and cannot be extended to those prerogatives which some particular cleric may enjoy by reason of an office, benefice, or assignment, which he holds. Thus it is manifest that the loose terminology of such a reputable author as Augustine cannot be sustained when he states without qualification that the prerogatives retained by a deposed cleric are all those mentioned in the second title of the second book of the Code (*De iuribus et privilegiis clericorum, canons* 118-123).[62] By inference, therefore, according to Augustine's statement, one would deduce that a cleric perpetually deprived of his garb loses not only the privileges common to all clerics as clerics, but also all those prerogatives which he had by reason of the office or benefice which he may previously have held. Such a conclusion would be manifestly erroneous, for these prerogatives have already been lost through the penalty of deposition which was previously inflicted. Likewise the content of canon 123 cannot be included under the listing of those privileges which are retained by a deposed cleric and lost by a perpetually defrocked cleric, since this canon does not enumerate any privileges, but speaks rather of the renunciation, loss, and recuperation of the privileges already listed. What is intended as an effect of deprivation of the clerical garb is a penal suspension or actual loss of the four common clerical privileges mentioned in canons 119-122 of the Code.

---

[62] Cf. *Commentary*, VIII, 260.

As a final remark regarding this effect of the penalty in question, it may be noted once again, as it already has been noted in the historical synopsis, that this is a change in the law. Before the promulgation of the Code, the only way in which these privileges could be lost was through the infliction of real degradation.[63]

Section 6. Effect on the Reception of the Sacraments

In the first section of this article, it was pointed out that any act of orders placed by a defrocked cleric (except when exercised in favor of a person who is in danger of death) would be illicit. It was also pointed out that (with the same exception) acts of jurisdiction when placed by a temporarily defrocked cleric are illicit, and that acts when placed by a cleric perpetually deprived of his garb are invalid. Accordingly, it presents no problem to state apodictically that a cleric hampered with this penalty is forbidden to be the active subject in the confection and administration of the sacraments, since to function thus requires the placing of acts of orders and jurisdiction,[64] which very acts a defrocked cleric is forbidden to place under pain of illicitness or nullity as the case may be.[65] Thus Prümmer (1866-1931), citing one specific instance of this general prohibition, stated that a cleric temporarily deprived of his garb cannot say Mass even privately.[66]

A question arises, however, regarding the status of these same clerics in respect to the *reception* of the sacraments. Are they, in other words, because of the fact that they have been deprived of their right to wear the clerical garb, forbidden to receive the sacraments as well as to administer them? Since the reception of baptism and confirmation is prerequisite to the reception of any Order,[67] there is no problem as to whether or not the defrocked cleric can receive these two sacraments. These two sacraments imprint an indelible character on the soul of the recipient, and

[63] Cf. Wernz-Vidal, *Ius Canonicum,* VII, n. 352, fn. 147.

[64] Cf. canons 738, 741, 782, 802, 845, 871, 872, 938, 951, 1094.

[65] Canons 2300 and 2304, § 1, taken with 2303, § 1.

[66] Cf. *Manuale Iuris Canonici,* p. 669.

[67] Cf. canons 968, § 1; 974, § 1, 1°.

consequently cannot be received more than once.[68] That one time had of necessity to occur prior to the time when the defrocked cleric became a cleric. Likewise there is no question of whether or not the defrocked cleric can receive the sacrament of matrimony. As will be pointed out in the second article of the subsequent chapter, this penalty should be inflicted only on major clerics. Accordingly, the defrocked cleric will not be able to marry unless he receives a dispensation from the obligation of celibacy, which he assumed in virtue of his major orders,[69] and which he retains after being deprived of the garb, as was already pointed out. Nor will there be any question of the defrocked cleric's receiving further Orders, since the ordaining prelate will scarcely consider him a fit subject for ordination.[70] Neither need one be concerned with the sacrament of Extreme Unction, since this sacrament can be received only when a person is in danger of death from sickness or old age, at which time the defrocked cleric can obviously receive the sacrament, if he be repentant. Indeed he is bound not to neglect receiving it.[71] The practical aspect of the question obviously is concerned with the defrocked cleric's capacity to receive regularly the sacraments of penance and the Holy Eucharist. The canons which specifically treat of the penalty do not make any explicit reference to the matter. Neither do the authors. To the writer, however, it seems clear that, *positis ponendis,* such clerics can receive these sacraments as often as they please. In other words, a defrocked cleric could receive Holy Communion daily if he so pleased as long as he is in the state of grace, fasting from midnight, and has the proper intention. This is evident from the fact that, like any other Catholic, he remains bound by the precepts of paschal communion and annual confession,[72] with which obligations he has to comply even though his penalty of deprivation of his garb, since it is a vindicative penalty, need never be dispensed from.[73] Even a degraded cleric (who certainly is

[68] Canon 732, § 1.
[69] Canons 132, § 1; 1072.
[70] Cf. canon 973, §§ 1 and 3.
[71] Canons 940, 942, 944.
[72] Canons 859, § 1, and 906.
[73] Canon 2298, 9°, 11°, and canon 2286.

in a worse condition than a cleric who has been deprived of his garb, for the latter still retains the status of a cleric) can still receive the sacraments, provided all the ordinary requisites are fulfilled. All authors are in agreement on this point.[74] *A fortiori,* a defrocked cleric can do the same.

It should be noted, however, with regard to *perpetual* deprivation of the garb, that the cleric so punished may be hindered from receiving the sacraments because of some other penalty which he has also incurred. This may very well be the case, since deposition must always precede perpetual deprivation of the garb, and deposition is preceded by or accompanied with excommunication (in five of the ten cases in which its infliction is warranted)[75] or personal interdict,[76] both of which penalties hinder the reception of the sacraments.[77] Accordingly, the cleric perpetually shorn of his right to wear the ecclesiastical garb will in these five cases be hindered from receiving the sacraments, but only until such time when he has receded from his contumacy and has received absolution from the censure that bound him.[78]

---

[74] Cf. Coronata, *Institutiones,* IV, p. 275, n. 1836: "Clericus (depositus et degradatus) per se non arcetur a Sacramentorum perceptione"; Jombart, *Des Délits et des Peines,* p. 692, n. 1118: "Le clerc dégradé . . . moyenant les conditions ordinaires, la réception des sacrements ne lui est pas interdite"; Findlay, *Deposition and Degradation,* pp. 218-219; Lega, *De Delictis et Poenis,* pp. 281-282, n. 208, in nota.

[75] Canons 2314, § 1, nn. 1 and 2; 2320; 2322; 2350.

[76] Canon 2328.

[77] Canons 2257, § 1; 2260; 2268; 2275, 2°.

[78] Canon 2250, § 2.

CHAPTER IV

Active and Passive Subject of the Penalty

Article 1. Active Subject

In speaking of temporary deprivation of the clerical garb, the Code makes no explicit mention of the person or persons possessed of the power required for the infliction of this penalty. Such an omission, however, need not be the cause of undue concern. Since temporary deprivation of the clerical garb is a true canonical penalty, its infliction, like the infliction of any other canonical penalty, requires an act of jurisdiction in the external forum, and therefore it can be inflicted only by those who enjoy the use of jurisdiction in the external forum.[1] Accordingly, it is evident that all others who either totally lack the power of jurisdiction (e.g., the laity)[2] or who in possessing the power of jurisdiction are restricted for its authorized use to the internal forum alone (e.g., pastors) are incompetent to inflict this penalty on a delinquent cleric.[3] One must not conclude, however, that everyone enjoying jurisdiction in the external forum is empowered indiscriminately to inflict upon a delinquent cleric the deprivation of his clerical garb. It is a fundamental principle of canon law that the power of jurisdiction can be exercised directly only over those who are subjects of the one exercising the jurisdiction.[4] Ordinarily, therefore, the only one competent to inflict this penalty on a cleric is the cleric's proper ordinary or the superior of that ordinary. For example, a secular cleric could be deprived of his garb only by his own local ordinary or by the Pope, who enjoys

[1] Cf. Cappello, *Tractatus Canonico-Moralis de Censuris iuxta Codicem Iuris Canonici* (3. ed., Taurinorum Augustae: Marietti, 1933), p. 11, n. 10 (hereafter cited as *De Censuris*); Lega, *De Delictis et Poenis*, p. 149, n. 103.

[2] Canon 118: "Soli clerici possunt potestatem . . . iurisdictionis ecclesiasticae . . . obtinere."

[3] Cf. Cappello, *De Censuris*, n. 10.

[4] Canon 201, § 1.

supreme jurisdiction over all the faithful.[5] The only other ordinaries subordinate to the Sovereign Pontiff whom one could imagine as being similarly competent are the ordinary of some territory, other than the delinquent cleric's own, where the cleric had perpetrated a delict, and the ordinary who is the delinquent's metropolitan. In the first assumption, the ordinary of the place where the delict was committed, together with the offender's proper ordinary, acquires a concurrent jurisdiction over the delinquent.[6] In the second assumption, one could imagine either the case wherein the cleric has committed a delict which calls for the deprivation of his garb, and the cognizance taken of this delict was coupled in some way with the visitation of a negligent suffragan's diocese by a metropolitan who had been properly empowered by the Holy See to conduct such a visitation,[7] or the case wherein the delinquent has appealed from his own ordinary's tribunal to that of the metropolitan against the sentence that inflicted the deprivation of his ecclesiastical garb.[8] Thus it is evident that the one who will ordinarily be the active subject for the infliction of a temporary deprivation of the wearing of a cleric's garb will be the delinquent's proper ordinary. This statement is borne out by the fact that the Code, in speaking of the infliction of *perpetual* deprivation of a cleric's garb, expressly states that it is the cleric's ordinary who is to inflict the penalty.[9] It now remains to see just who are comprehended under this term "ordinary."

The ordinary empowered by the law of the Code to inflict deprivation of the clerical garb may be any one of those who are enumerated under canon 198 of the Code. Accordingly, this penalty may be inflicted by residential bishops,[10] apostolic administrators,[11]

---

[5] Cf. Ryan, *Principles of Episcopal Jurisdiction,* The Catholic University of America Canon Law Studies, n. 120 (Washington, D. C.: Catholic University of America Press, 1939), p. 97.

[6] Canon 1566, § 1: "Ratione delicti reus forum sortitur in loco patrati delicti."

[7] Canon 274, 5°; cf. also Roberti, *De Delictis in Genere,* p. 78.

[8] Canons 274, 7°, and 1594, § 1; cf. also Roberti, *loc. cit.*

[9] Canon 2304: "Si clericus . . . *Ordinarius* potest eum perpetuo privare iure deferendi habitum ecclesiasticum."

[10] Canons 329, § 1; 334, § 1; and 335, § 1.

[11] Canons 312, 315, §§ 1 and 2, 1°.

vicars and prefects apostolic,[12] abbots and prelates who rule over autonomous and independent territories,[13] cathedral chapters (the diocesan consultors in the United States), but only during the interregnum after the death of the bishop and before the election of the vicar capitular (in the United States, the administrator),[14] the vicar capitular (administrator in the United States) appointed to govern the vacant see,[15] and the major superiors and general chapters in exempt clerical religious institutes.[16] The following are major superiors: (a) the abbot primate, (b) the abbot superior of a monastic congregation (these first two, however, do not enjoy this power of jurisdiction over the monks of all the abbeys in the order or congregation unless it is expressly granted to them by the constitutions or by a decree of the Holy See), (c) the abbot of an independent monastery, (d) the supreme moderator, (e) the provincial, and (f) the vicar and anyone who has power after the fashion of a provincial.[17] The powers of local superiors to inflict canonical penalties must be determined from the constitutions of the clerical religious institute in question.[18]

A final word may be added here concerning the power of the vicar-general to inflict this penalty. While it is true that the vicar-general is listed among those who are included in the term "ordinary," it must be remembered that canon 198 states that all those listed therein are to be considered as ordinaries unless one or the other of them is expressly excepted in regard to some particular power of ordinaries.[19] Such an explicit exception is made with regard to the vicar-general when the infliction of a penalty (such as deprivation of a cleric's garb) is the power of the ordinary which is in question. In this instance, the vicar-general requires a special mandate.[20]

---

[12] Canons 293, § 1 and 294, § 1.

[13] Canons 319, § 1 and 323, § 1.

[14] Canons 427 and 435, § 1.

[15] Canon 435, § 1.

[16] Canons 488, 2°, 4°, and 501, § 1.

[17] Canon 488, 8°.

[18] Cf. Roberti, *De Delictis in Genere*, p. 79, n. 56.

[19] Canon 198, § 1: "In iure nomine *Ordinarii* intelliguntur, nisi quis expresse excipiatur, . . ."

[20] Canon 2220, § 2: "Vicarius Generalis sine mandato speciali non habet potestatem infligendi poenas."

Theoretically, then, all the ecclesiastics listed above are capable of being the active subject with regard to the infliction of the penalty in question. Which one will become the active subject in a particular case depends on who and where is the cleric who is to be the passive subject. Practically, however, in almost all cases the real active subject will be a judge or a collegiate body of judges delegated by the proper ordinary for the hearing of a particular case. The truth of this statement will be apparent when the infliction of this penalty is treated *ex professo* in the following chapter of this dissertation. For the present it suffices to state that the power of those mentioned above for the inflicting of this penalty is an ordinary power; as such it could be delegated to others and in the present instance (since there is question of a criminal trial) it is highly recommended that it be so delegated.[21]

ARTICLE 2. PASSIVE SUBJECT

Theoretically, *any* cleric, whether constituted in major or in minor orders, or simply as a member of the clerical state by reason of his reception of first tonsure, is liable to the penalty of temporary or perpetual deprivation of his clerical garb provided all the conditions postulated for the infliction of so severe a penalty are verified in his particular case. In practice, however, with regard to incorrigible scandalous conduct on the part of clerics who have not as yet received any major orders, the delinquent's superior, without invoking even the temporary form of the penalty in question, should by means of an administrative decree reduce the offending minor cleric to the lay state immediately as an unfit subject for promotion to sacred orders. Such action is provided for in canon 211, § 2, of the Code.[22] Such a decree of reduction to the lay state, moreover, achieves the same effects as deprivation of the minor cleric's garb, since it carries with it a prohibition to wear the ecclesiastical garb or tonsure and an automatic loss of the clerical privileges.[23]

[21] Cf. canons 197, § 1; 199, § 1; 2220, § 1; 1578.

[22] "Clericus minor ad statum laicalem regreditur. . . . Ordinarii (loci) decreto iusta de causa lato, si nempe Ordinarius, omnibus perpensis, prudenter iudicaverit clericum non posse cum decore status clericalis ad ordines sacros promoveri." Cf. Blat, *Commentarium,* V, p. 183, n. 133.

[23] Canon 213, § 1.

If, however, the minor cleric in question be in addition a professed member of some religious community, the process is not as simple. Canon 211, § 2, explicitly states that it is the *local* ordinary who is given this power of reducing by decree a minor cleric to the lay state when for a just cause he prudently conjectures that the cleric cannot be promoted to sacred orders without detriment to the dignity of the clerical state. In virtue of an explicit provision in the Code, religious major superiors are expressly excluded from the ambit embraced by the term *"Ordinarius loci."*[24] Consequently, a minor cleric who is at the same time a professed religious cannot be reduced to the lay state simply by means of a decree issued by his proper ordinary in virtue of canon 211, § 2. In the case of such a cleric, the proper procedure called for would be the expulsion of the cleric from the religious state. Once the minor cleric had been lawfully dismissed from his religious institute, he automatically would be reduced to the lay state by a special provision of the common law of the Code.[25] Briefly, the dismissal of the offending minor cleric from his religious institute, which dismissal carries with it an automatic reduction to the lay state, would be carried out in the following manner. In the case of a clerical exempt religious community, or of a clerical community which though non-exempt enjoys pontifical approval, the superior who could so act would be the superior-general or the abbot of a monastery *sui iuris* with the consent of his council manifested by secret ballot, provided the cleric to be dismissed is only in temporary vows.[26] If he be in perpetual vows, then in the case of a clerical exempt institute, his dismissal could be effected only by means of a judicial sentence handed down by a collegiate tribunal of five judges, which sentence must be

[24] Canon 198, § 1: "In iure nomine *Ordinarii* intelliguntur, nisi qui expresse excipiatur, praeter Romanum Pontificem, pro suo quisque territorio Episcopus residentialis, Abbas vel Praelatus *nullius* eorumque Vicarius Generalis, Administrator, Vicarius et Praefectus Apostolicus, itemque ii qui praedictis deficientibus interim ex iuris praescripto aut ex probatis constitutionibus succedunt in regimine, pro suis vero subditis Superiores maiores in religionibus clericalibus exemptis. § 2: Nomine autem *Ordinarii loci* seu *locorum* veniunt omnes recensiti, exceptis Superioribus religiosis."

[25] Canons 648 and 669, § 2.

[26] Canon 647, § 1.

confirmed by the Holy See.[27] In the case of a clerical non-exempt institute which has pontifical approval, the dismissal of such a cleric would have to result through an administrative decree of the superior-general with the consent of his council, which decree must be confirmed by the Holy See.[28] In the case of a clerical non-exempt institute of diocesan approval only, for the dismissal of a minor cleric in temporary vows a decree of the local ordinary would be sufficient, provided he had informed the religious superior of the minor cleric in question, and the superior had no just reason for withholding consent.[29] For the dismissal of a minor cleric professed with perpetual vows in this last type of institute, a decree of the local ordinary again would be sufficient after he had obtained the consent of the superior-general, who in turn must have obtained the majority vote of his council for the dismissal.[30] For the dismissal of a minor cleric in temporary vows the Code demands that there must be a grave cause, e.g., the absence of a religious spirit which has proved scandalous to the other members of the institute and has not been amended after repeated admonitions and penances.[31] For the dismissal of a minor cleric in perpetual vows, the Code postulates on the part of the delinquent that he be guilty of three delicts, or of one which is virtually triple because of the lack of emendation after due warning. At least two warnings must have been given in vain.[32] Since incorrigibility is the very reason why temporary or perpetual deprivation of the garb is inflicted upon a cleric, it is readily seen that no injustice is being done to a minor cleric professed in some religious institute when the legitimate superior chooses to dismiss him from the institute rather than to merely deprive him of his garb, since he is guilty of the very offense, namely incorrigibility, which the Code deems of sufficient gravity for his legitimate dismissal.

A difficulty is encountered, however, with regard to the automatic

[27] Canons 664, 665, 666, and 1576, § 1, 2°.

[28] Canon 650, §§ 1 and 2, 2°.

[29] Canon 647, § 1.

[30] Canon 650, §§ 1 and 2, 1°.

[31] Canon 647, § 2, 1° and 2°.

[32] Canons 649, 656-662.

reduction to the lay state which in virtue of canon 648 is consequent upon the legitimate dismissal of minor clerics who are religious professed with temporary vows. The problem consists in this: does the provision of canon 648 apply to clerics religious when they received their minor orders as secular clerics prior to their entrance into the religious institute as well as to clerics religious who received their minor orders in the institute itself? There are some authors who maintain that either type of cleric is automatically reduced to the lay state upon his legitimate dismissal from the institute.[33] Others maintain that only those minor clerics religious who actually received minor orders in the institute are automatically reduced to the lay state upon their legitimate dismissal.[34] The main reason advanced by this second school of thought for their opinion is that the minor cleric religious who received his minor orders prior to his entrance into religion does not lose his diocese of incardination until perpetual profession,[35] and it does not seem just that the cleric's bishop should be deprived of the cleric's services merely because he is dismissed from the religious institute by his religious superior for a reason which, while it may be indicative of the cleric's unfitness for the *religious* state, may in no wise be indicative of his unfitness for the *clerical* state. Of course if the latter unfitness were also present, then the cleric's local ordinary could avail himself of the power granted him by canon 211, § 2. This second opinion, in the opinion of the present writer, appears more tenable.[36] In the supposition that the cleric has been dismissed from his institute because of his

[33] Cf., e.g., O'Neill, *The Dismissal of Religious in Temporary Vows,* Catholic University of America Canon Law Studies, n. 166 (Washington, D. C.: Catholic University of America Press, 1942), p. 149.

[34] Cf., e.g., Goyeneche, "Consultatio," *Commentarium pro Religiosis et Missionariis* (formerly, i.e., prior to 1935, *Commentarium pro Religiosis*), XIX (1938), 163-166; Schäfer, *Compendium de Religiosis ad Normam Codicis Iuris Canonici* (3. ed., Romae: S.A.L.E.R., 1940), p. 1000; Sweeney, *The Reduction of Clerics to the Lay State,* pp. 76-79.

[35] Canon 585.

[36] For a more extensive presentation of the arguments pro and con, the reader may consult the works already cited. Further discussion of the matter will not add anything to the question at hand, viz., the advisability of substituting reduction to the lay state by way of decree or by way of dismissal from the religious institute in place of deprivation of the clerical garb when the culprit is in minor orders only.

unfitness for the religious state, with no corresponding unfitness for the clerical state, it must be noted, however, that the cleric's local ordinary must have recourse to the Sacred Congregation of Seminaries and Universities to obtain judgment in the case before he can readmit the cleric in question to a seminary to be ordained for his diocese. This is in accord with a joint decree of the Sacred Congregation of Religious and the Sacred Congregation of Seminaries and Universities, issued on July 25, 1941.[37]

The problem does not arise with regard to minor clerics who are legitimately dismissed after making profession of *perpetual* vows. In that supposition, even though the religious in question received minor orders as a secular cleric before entering the religious institute, he has lost his diocese of incardination by reason of the perpetual profession,[38] and consequently is subject to the same general provision of canon 669, § 2, i.e., he is automatically reduced to the lay state upon his legitimate dismissal from the religious institute just the same as any other minor cleric religious would be if he had received his minor orders in the institute itself.

With regard to the reduction of minor clerics secular through the administrative decree authorized in canon 211, § 2, it is to be noted that the local ordinary so empowered is the ordinary of the diocese in which the offending cleric is incardinated. The only exception to this rule would occur in the case wherein the minor cleric committed a delict against the sixth commandment in the diocese of some ordinary other than his own proper one. In this case, if the circumstances warrant it, the cleric can be reduced to the lay state, and the competent forum attaches to the place where the delict was committed.[39] This power, it must be noted

[37] *AAS,* XXXIII (1941), 371; Bouscaren, *The Canon Law Digest* (2 vols. and supplement through 1948, Milwaukee: Bruce, 1934, 1943, 1949), II, 426.

[38] Canon 585: "Professus a votis perpetuis sive solemnibus sive simplicibus amittit ipso iure propriam quam in saeculo habebat dioecesim"; cf. Sweeney, *The Reduction of Clerics to the Lay State,* p. 86.

[39] Cf. Sweeney, *The Reduction of Clerics to the Lay State,* p. 116; canon 2358: "Clerici in minoribus ordinibus constituti, rei alicuius delicti contra sextum decalogi praeceptum, pro gravitate culpae puniantur etiam dimissione e statu clericali, si delicti adiuncta id suadeant, . . ."; canon 1566, § 1: "Ratione delicti reus forum sortitur in loco patrati delicti."

however, is ordinary power, and can be delegated to other responsible persons for possible use when the necessary conditions are verified in a particular case. Thus a local ordinary who has his seminarians trained in a seminary which is located in a diocese other than his own may see fit to delegate the power acknowledged to him in canon 211, § 2, to the superiors of the seminary, to be used whenever they find it necessary to dismiss one of the minor clerics incardinated in his diocese.[40]

One should also bear in mind that there are cited in the Code several instances wherein a cleric not yet in major orders becomes *ipso facto* reduced to the lay state apart from all necessary issuance of any decree on the part of the local ordinary. Such an *ipso facto* ensuing reduction, as well as the reduction by way of decree, is accompanied with an automatic loss of the clerical privileges and a prohibition that bars the cleric from wearing his distinctive dress or his tonsure.[41] *Ipso facto* ensuing reduction to the lay state is decreed by the Code for a minor cleric who contracts a marriage, provided that it be not invalid by reason of force or fear;[42] who lays aside freely and without legitimate reason his clerical garb and does not resume the wearing of it within a month after having been duly warned;[43] or who voluntarily enlists in the armed forces without the permission of his lawful Superior.[44] All of these causes, as Findlay is careful to point out, "are consonant with his (the minor cleric's) freedom to return to

[40] Cf. Sweeney, *op. cit.*, pp. 116-118; canons 197, § 1; 199, § 1.

[41] Canon 213, § 1.

[42] Canon 132, § 2: "Clerici minores possunt quidem nuptias inire, sed, nisi matrimonium fuerit nullum vi aut metu eisdem incusso, ipso iure e statu clericali decidunt." Cf. also Sweeney, *op. cit.*, pp. 46-55.

[43] Canon 136, § 3: "Clerici minores qui propria auctoritate sine legitima causa habitum ecclesiasticum et tonsuram dimiserint, nec, ab Ordinario moniti, sese intra mensem emendaverint, ipso iure e statu clericali decidunt." Cf. also Sweeney, *op. cit.*, pp. 55-64; cf. also canon 2379.

[44] Canon 141, § 1: "Saecularem militiam ne capessant voluntarii, nisi cum sui Ordinarii licentia, ut citius liberi evadant, id fecerint; . . . § 2. Clericus minor qui contra praescriptum § 1 sponte sua militiae nomen dederit, ipso iure e statu clericali decidit." Cf. Sweeney, *op. cit.*, pp. 64-69; 83.

the state of the laity. They are causes which create a presumption of his renunciation of the clerical state. . . .[45]

Besides these *ipso facto* ensuing reductions to the lay state for minor clerics, and in addition to the administrative processes already described, the Code makes mention of two cases wherein reduction to the lay state is inflicted upon minor clerics *as a penalty* for the commission of certain delicts. Canon 2358, for example, allows for the infliction of such a penalty, when the circumstances warrant it, as the punishment of a minor cleric guilty of some delict against the sixth commandment. Canon 2387 demands the infliction of the same penalty in the case of a minor cleric religious whose profession is declared null because of *dolus* perpetrated by the cleric.[46] In the first of these two instances, the cleric's proper ordinary or the ordinary of the place where the delict was committed may see fit to inflict the penalty indicated, viz., reduction to the lay state, rather than to merely inflict deprivation of the cleric's garb which, as has already been pointed out, would still leave the culprit a member of the clerical state, though shorn of his clerical privileges and deprived of his right to wear a distinctive garb. If the ordinary should choose so to act, there would be no necessity of his also inflicting the penalty of depriva-

---

[45] Cf. *Deposition and Degradation,* p. 209; cf. also Sweeney, *op. cit.,* p. 46: ". . . once the minor cleric places an act which, according to law, calls for an immediate return to the lay state, he loses the clerical state. The placing of this act is not necessarily a delict, though it can be such, nor is it necessarily a prohibited act, though again it may be such. Since the cleric himself performs the act, the principal cause of the reduction is the will of the cleric. Hence this method of reduction is rather termed a return to the lay state or a fall from the clerical state. Considered as an operation of law it may be regarded as a reduction in which the law itself is the effective agent of it, and so this operation is included under the general title in the Code, '*De reductione clericorum ad statum laicalem.*' However, in the canons themselves which speak of this reduction, the phrase, 'fall from the clerical state,' is used. Consequently, in these canons it is evident that the agent is considered rather from the side of the person who places the act. In the three canons which treat of this method of reduction this terminology is consistently used."

[46] "Religiosus clericus cuius professio ob admissum ab ipso dolum nulla fuerit declarata, si sit in minoribus ordinibus constitutus, e statu clericali abiiciatur. . . ."

tion of the cleric's garb, since the prohibition against ever wearing the garb once reduction to the lay state has occurred would automatically be in force.[47] Neither would there be any necessity of inflicting deprivation of the clerical garb in the case of the minor cleric religious whose profession was declared null because of fraud perpetrated by the religious himself. The only difference in this case would be that the superior must inflict the penalty of reduction to the lay state once the fact of fraud is verified and the profession has been declared null, since the prescription of canon 2387 is stated in preceptive words. The prohibition enacted in canon 213, § 1, thereupon would automatically obtain.

From the foregoing discussion it is clear that deprivation of the clerical garb, when the circumstances calling for its infliction are present in a particular case, should be employed only with respect to clerics in major orders. With regard to those major clerics, however, who have received the fullness of the priesthood by reason of episcopal consecration, or who have been honored with the cardinalitial dignity before ordination to the priesthood, or who have been honored by their appointment as legates of the Holy See, it must be remembered that, if there arose any case that involved a possible deprivation of the garb in their regard, it would be reserved by the common law of the Code to the judgment of the Roman Pontiff himself, and therefore could not be subjected to the same procedure as that which is outlined in the following chapter of this dissertation.[48] Any emerging case

[47] Canon 213, § 1: "Omnes qui e clericali statu ad laicalem legitime redacti aut regressi sunt, eo ipso amittunt officia, beneficia, iura ac privilegia clericalia et vetantur in habitu ecclesiastico incedere ac tonsuram deferre." Cf. also Sweeney, *op. cit.,* pp. 89-109, especially pp. 93-94 where he discusses the question of whether or not the penalty of reduction to the lay state implies the penalty of deprivation of the clerical garb. He holds that it does not, and with good reason. Otherwise, reduction to the lay state and degradation would be one and the same penalty. What he does not point out is the fact that the prohibition contained in canon 213, § 1, obviates the necessity of inflicting a deprivation of the garb.

[48] Cf. canons 1557, § 1: "Ipsius Romani Pontificis dumtaxat ius est iudicandi: . . . 2°. Patres Cardinales; 3°. Legatos Sedis Apostolicae, et in criminalibus Episcopos, etiam titulares," and 2227, § 1: "Poena nonnisi a Romano Pontifice infligi aut declarari potest in eos de quibus in can. 1557, § 1."

wherein the infliction of deprivation of the clerical garb would be indicated as the proper remedy to be taken would, if it concerned one of these major clerics, be a major cause[49] reserved to the Roman Pontiff in such a manner that every other judge or tribunal in the Church is absolutely incompetent.[50] Any action taken against this privileged class of clerics, therefore, by any other than the Roman Pontiff himself or his delegate would be invalid.[51] According to Roberti, the reservation of these causes is apparently founded on the episcopal character.[52] While the Pope alone, however, is competent to pass sentence on these persons, he will usually delegate the cause to one of the congregations or to a commission of cardinals.[53]

Indeed the Council of Trent, having made the supposition that a cause might arise which of its nature would demand that it be entrusted by the Pope to others than those already mentioned, stated that such causes could be committed not only to the Roman Curia but also to metropolitans or bishops outside the Curia chosen by the Pope with a special commission signed by his own hand. The Council added, however, that such causes were to be committed to no others than the ones selected, and that the commission extended simply to the power of drawing up in due procedural form an organized report, which the ones who were thus delegated were to transmit immediately to the Roman Pontiff, who in turn alone was competent to pass the definitive sentence.[54] Strictly, however, the Pope could commit these major causes to judges outside the Roman Curia other than metropolitans and bishops; could delegate these judges even for the pronouncement of the sentence; could delegate them to review the cause and terminate it even within the Roman Curia; could set up judges

[49] Canon 220: "Gravioris momenti negotia quae uni Romano Pontifici reservantur sive natura sua, sive positiva lege, *causae maiores* appellantur."

[50] Canon 1558: "In causis de quibus in can. 1556, 1557, aliorum iudicum incompetentia est *absoluta.*"

[51] Canon 1892: "Sententia vitio insanabilis nullitatis laborat, quando: 1°. Lata est a iudice absolute incompetente vel. . . ."

[52] Cf. *De Processibus,* Vol. I (2. ed., Romae: apud Aedes Facultatis Iuridicae ad S. Apollinaris, 1941), p. 184, n. 63.

[53] Cf. Roberti, *loc. cit.*

[54] Sess. XXIV, *de ref.,* c. 5.

and tribunals endowed with ordinary jurisdiction over the causes of these special classes of clerics.[55] Likewise the Pope, if he chose so to act, was not required to expressly derogate the legislation of the Tridentine Fathers, since they themselves declared that the decrees of the Council were to be understood in conformity with the authority enjoyed by the Holy See.[56]

Because of the supreme jurisdiction which he enjoys as the Sovereign Pontiff, the Pope is free either to observe the formalities laid down in the law or not to do so. If he should decide to accommodate himself to the procedure established by ecclesiastical law, he is said to proceed by ordinary law. Such formal procedure, however, would not be necessary for the validity of his action. In order that his action be licit, however, the natural law demands that he deprive a bishop, cardinal, or apostolic legate, of his garb only for a proportionately grave cause, such as the reasons given in the Code for the same action with reference to other major clerics.[57]

As to deprivation of the clerical garb with reference to the Pope himself as the passive subject, there can be no question. The Roman Pontiff, in virtue of his divinely given primacy, is not subject to the coercive power of any human authority; he is subject solely to the power and the judgment of God.[58] The truth of this statement is evident not only from the very nature of the primacy, but also from the undeviating tradition and practice of the Church, which has ever taught that the primatial See of Rome transcends all human judgment.[59] This constant doctrine

---

[55] Cf. Bouix, *Tractatus de Episcopo ubi et de Synodo Dioecesana* (2. ed., Parisiis, 1873), I, 323-330.

[56] Conc. Trident., sess. XXV, *de ref.*, c. 21.

[57] Cf. Smith, *Elements of Ecclesiastical Law* (3 vols., New York, 1877-93), II (3. ed. 1888), pp. 172-173, n. 405; Cocchi, *Commentarium*, II, pp. 223-224, n. 269.

[58] Cf. canon 218, §§ 1 and 2; c. 13, X, *de iudiciis*, II, 1; c. 6, X, *de electione et electi potestate*, I, 6; Wernz, *Ius Decretalium*, II, p. 697, n. 617.

[59] Cf. c. 4, 5, 7, 9, D. XXI; c. 7, 10-12, 15, D. XCVI; c. 10, 13-17, C. IX, q. 3; c. 30, C. XVII, q. 4; c. 12, X, *de iudiciis*, II, 1; c. 1, *de maioritate et obedientia*, I, 8, in Extravag. comm.; IV, Conc. Constantinopolitan, actio X, can. 21—*Fontes*, n. 6; Conc. Vatican., sess. IV, c. III, *de vi et ratione primatus Romani Pontificis*—*Fontes*, n. 10; S. Zosimus, ep. *Quamvis Patrum traditio*, 21 mart. 418—*Fontes*, n. 21; S. Bonifacius I, ep. *Retro maioribus*

has been repeated and epitomized in the law of the Code.[60]

A final word may be added with regard to the possibility of inflicting this penalty upon Oriental clerics. Since members of the various Oriental rites in general are not bound by the penalties of the Latin Code, except in those cases wherein a delict has been perpetrated concerning which the Holy Office is competent, Oriental clerics are not included among the passive subjects of this penalty.[61]

By way of summary it may be stated that the proper potential passive subject of this penalty is any major cleric of the Latin rite, to the exclusion of course of the Roman Pontiff. Moreover, in the cases of bishops, cardinals, and apostolic legates, there must also be observed the special provisions that touch the requisite juridical procedure.

---

tuis, 11 mart. 422—*Fontes,* n. 22; S. Leo IX, *ep. In terra pax hominibus,* 2 sept. 1053, c. 32—*Fontes,* n. 27; Ioannes XXII, const. *Licet,* 23 oct. 1327, art. 3, errorum Marsilii Patavini et Ioannis de Ianduno damn.—*Fontes,* n. 38; Clemens VI, ep. *Super quibusdam,* 29 sept. 1351—*Fontes,* n. 42; Paulus IV, const. *Cum ex Apostolatus,* 15 febr. 1559, § 1—*Fontes,* n. 94; Pius IX, Syllabus Errorum, prop. 34, 41—*Fontes,* n. 543; Pius IX, const. *Apostolicae Sedis,* 12 oct. 1869, § I, n. 4; § VI, n. 1—*Fontes,* n. 552; Leo XIII, const. *Romanos Pontifices,* 8 maii 1881—*Fontes,* n. 582; Leo XIII, allocut. *Mirandum sane,* 1 iun. 1888, § 5—*Fontes,* n. 599.

[60] Canon 1556: "Prima Sedes a nemine iudicatur."

[61] Cf. canons 1, 247, ¶ 2 and 257, § 2; Roberti, *De Delictis in Genere,* p. 80, n. 57.

CHAPTER V

Infliction of the Penalty

ARTICLE 1. INFLICTION OF TEMPORARY DEPRIVATION OF THE CLERICAL GARB

Section 1. Prerequisites

The ordinary cannot legitimately proceed to punish a cleric with temporary deprivation of his clerical garb without the observance of certain prerequisites. Canon 2300 lists three conditions which must be verified before the penalty in question can be invoked. First of all, the ordinary must ascertain that the cleric to be so punished is actually guilty of gravely scandalous conduct.[1] Secondly, the cleric must have been admonished to desist from such conduct and then be guilty of paying no heed to the admonition given.[2] Finally, there must be no other way in which the scandal can be removed.[3] All three of these conditions must be simultaneously present before this grave penalty can be inflicted.[4] Before proceeding to discuss the actual infliction of this penalty once the concurrent existence of these three conditions has been verified, however, one may with profit give consideration to each one of these prerequisites in particular.

With regard to the scandal that is postulated, one may note that in the text of the Code this word is rendered both by the plural *"scandala"* and by the singular *"scandalum."* Because of the use of the plural number in the Code with reference to the scandal required on the part of the delinquent, some authors maintain that one isolated instance of scandal on the part of a cleric would not constitute a sufficient reason for the infliction of this penalty. Augustine, for example, maintained that "diverse

[1] "Si clericus gravia scandala praebeat. . . ."

[2] ". . . et monitus non resipiscat, . . ."

[3] ". . . nec scandalum queat aliter removeri, . . ."

[4] Cf. Wernz-Vidal, *Ius Canonicum,* VII, p. 367, n. 349, V.

or protracted or repeated scandals" may be meant as the object of this penalty.[5] In a similar fashion, Salucci stated that the scandal needed to be repeated and continued for a certain period of time.[6] Perhaps that is what is meant, but one could just as easily argue that the commission of a single scandalous act (provided that it was gravely scandalous) constituted reason enough for the infliction of this penalty, since the singular number is used in the text with reference to the third prerequisite (namely, that temporary deprivation of the garb be the *"unicum remedium"* whereby the scandal can be removed. More important than the question of whether or not a single act of scandal constituted a sufficient reason for the infliction of this penalty is the question of what gravity is postulated for the scandal given. Wernz-Vidal were careful to point out that the scandal which is to be punished in this manner needed to be a grave scandal.[7] Accordingly, an ordinary could not inflict temporary deprivation of the garb for some delictual conduct or demeanor which could be considered scandalous only in a broad fashion. For example, a course of action on the part of a cleric which might seem highly scandalous to a few people of prurient mind would seem only imprudent or indecorous to many others possessed of a keener insight into the foibles of human nature. How is the superior to determine whether or not in a given case actual and grave scandal has been given? It is rather difficult to set up a universal norm as to the number and kind of people who need to be scandalized by the cleric's conduct before an ordinary can inflict temporary deprivation of the cleric's garb. To the writer, however, it seems that a practical norm could be obtained from an analogy with the norm set up in the Code for the determination of infamy of fact. In other words, the ordinary would be right in determining that the postulated scandal is present when the cleric, either because of some certain delict which he has committed or because of his depraved conduct, has lost his good reputation with righteous

---

[5] Cf. *Commentary,* VIII, 259, fn. 11.

[6] Cf. *Il Diritto Penale secondo il Codice di Diritto Canonico* (2 vols. in 1, Subiaco, 1926-1930), I, 318 (hereafter cited as *Il Diritto Penale*).

[7] Cf. *Ius Canonicum, loc. cit.*

and serious Catholics.[8] The designation of this specific norm seems even more felicitous when one considers that in the canon which immediately follows the one just cited it is explicitly stated that one who is infamous in fact is to be restrained from exercising the sacred ministry.[9] A similar prohibition to exercise any ecclesiastical ministry accompanies the infliction of a temporary deprivation of the garb.[10] Hence it seems that a fair criterion for the ordinary to employ when judging whether the postulated scandal has been given is the ascertainment whether the cleric in question has lost his good reputation among those members of the faithful whom he (the ordinary) judges to be righteous and serious. While he does not expressly cite the norm set down in the Code for the determination of infamy of fact, Blat (+1943) seemed to adopt this norm as the one to be used by the ordinary in cases of clerical scandal, for he utilized a terminology with regard to his commentary on canon 2300 which is very similar to that used in the Code with regard to the determination of infamy of fact.[11]

Relative to the second prerequisite (the warning that must be given to the delinquent cleric), the commentary of two authors in particular may be noted. Berutti identifies the *"monitio"* required by canon 2300 with the *"monitio"* listed among the penal remedies in canon 2306. This is evident from the fact that he refers his reader to canon 2309, § 5, which allows for the possibility of giving the *"monitio"* which is a penal remedy secretly as long as the fact that it was indeed given can be verified from a document which is kept in the secret archives of the diocesan curia.[12] Augustine refers his readers to the general norm set down in canon 2143 concerning the formalities to be observed when the giving of any warning is prescribed as the norm to be followed in the giving of this particular admonition.[13] Both authors, in the

[8] Cf. canon 2293, § 3: "Infamia facti contrahitur, quando quis, ob patratum delictum vel ob pravos mores, bonam existimationem apud fideles probos et graves amisit, de quo iudicium spectat ad Ordinarium."

[9] Canon 2294, § 2.

[10] Canon 2300.

[11] Cf. *Commentarium*, V, p. 183, n. 133.

[12] Cf. *De Delictis et Poenis*, p. 232, n. 89, 9°.

[13] Cf. *Commentary*, VIII, 259, fn. 10.

opinion of the writer, are correct in their assumptions. Accordingly, the following remarks on the procedure to be followed in the giving of this warning should be noted. The ordinary can, either personally or through the intervention of some third party, warn the delinquent cleric to amend his ways.[14] This warning can be made secretly (subject to the limitation pointed out above) or publicly.[15] If it be given publicly, then it should be given either orally in the presence of the chancellor or some other official of the curia (e.g., the vicar-general, the *officialis,* the promoter of justice, etc.) or before two witnesses, or by letter.[16] If the latter method be selected (e.g., because of the great distance from the curia to the place where the delinquent cleric lives), then the ordinary must be careful to select that form of correspondence which is safest and which guarantees a notification of the letter's reception.[17] In the United States a warning given by registered letter to be delivered to the addressee personally with a request for return receipt would fulfill these requirements.[18] No matter which method is chosen, however, for the giving of the public warning, an authentic document mentioning the fact that the warning was given together with the general tenor of the warning (i.e., the reasons why it was given and what penalty was threatened if the warning would go unheeded) should be kept in the secret archives of the diocese.[19] It should be noted that in the case under consideration the notary who draws up such an authentic document should be a priest.[20] If the warning be given in the presence of the chancellor of the curia, he could act as the notary, and thus the intervention of any other notary would no longer be required.[21] If the cleric should refuse to present himself in person to the ordinary so that the warning might be given orally, or if he refuses

---

[14] Canon 2307.

[15] Canon 2309, § 1.

[16] Canons 2309, § 2; 2143, § 1; 363, § 2.

[17] Canons 1719; 2309, § 2.

[18] Cf. Coronata, *Manuale Practicum Iuris Disciplinaris et Criminalis Regularium* (Taurini: Marietti, 1938), n. 30.

[19] Canons 2143, § 1; 2309, § 2 and 5.

[20] Canon 373, § 3.

[21] Canon 372, § 1 and 3.

to accept the letter which contains the warning, he is to be considered as warned.[22] The same would hold true if the delinquent cleric actually accepted the letter, but destroyed it without reading its contents.[23] The necessary warning can be given once only or several times according to the prudent judgment of the superior.[24] These, then are the elements that attend the warning which is required in virtue of canon 2300.

Concerning the third prerequisite which must be verified before the superior can proceed to deprive temporarily a cleric of his garb (viz., the fact that there exists no other possible way in which to rectify the situation), not much need be said. Perhaps one should here indicate what other possible remedies the superior could avail himself of. First and foremost, if the prerequisite warning has been given in vain, there seems to be reason for the employment of another of the penal remedies listed in canon 2306, viz., the precept. The ordinary in detailed fashion should embody in this precept, not only those things which the delinquent cleric is to do, but also those things which he is to avoid, and should fortify the precept with the threat of a penalty to be inflicted if the precept is transgressed.[25] To this precept may be added the penal remedy of surveillance if the gravity of the case warrants such action.[26]

Another possibility lies at hand for the ordinary. He may inflict upon the delinquent cleric one or the other of the various ecclesiastical penances. The Code allows the imposition of various penances in the external forum (as long as the transgression so punished is public, which it certainly is in the case in question because of the scandal given) in order to afford the delinquent an opportunity to escape the infliction of a graver penalty (e.g., temporary deprivation of his clerical garb).[27] Indeed, the ordinary could impose such a penance at the same time that he gives the necessary admonition if he deems such a course of action prudent.[28]

---

[22] Canon 2143, § 3.
[23] Cf. Coronata, *Institutiones,* III (3. ed., 1948), 506.
[24] Canon 2309, § 6,
[25] Canon 2310.
[26] Canon 2311, § 1.
[27] Canon 2312, § 1 and 2.
[28] Canon 2313, § 2.

One such penance which seems particularly apropos in the case of a cleric guilty of scandalous conduct could derive from the command that he undertake a retreat in some pious or religious house for a certain length of time.[29] When such penal remedies and penances have been tried and found wanting, the ordinary may consider the infliction of one of the lesser vindicative penalties, such as suspension for a certain length of time, or penal translation from the cleric's present office or benefice to one of inferior rank, or relegation to a clerical house of penance for a certain period of time.[30] If, however, in the opinion of the ordinary, even the infliction of these lesser vindicative penalties would prove of no avail, then he may proceed to the actual infliction of the penalty in question.

Section 2. Infliction of the Penalty

For the infliction of a temporary deprivation of the clerical garb Coronata and other reputable canonists assert that no special procedure is necessary, since the Code itself describes the procedure by requiring that a warning threatening the penalty be given prior to the actual infliction of it. The warning itself, however, is of absolute necessity.[31] This view is not without its difficulties. Accordingly a fuller treatment of the procedure to be followed in the infliction of this penalty is in order. Wernz-Vidal in their commentary on the warning required by canon 2300 make reference to the provision set down in canon 2222, § 1, for the punishment of transgressions of ecclesiastical laws which have no explicit penal sanction attached to them.[32]

---

[29] Canon 2313, § 1, 5°.

[30] Canons 2298, 2°, 3°, 8°; 2301; 2302; cf. also Berutti, *De Delictis et Poenis,* 232, n. 89, 9°.

[31] Cf. *Institutiones,* IV, p. 272, n. 1832: "Nulla specialis procedura necessaria est, cum Codex ipse proceduram describat per monitionem. Monitio tamen est absolute necessaria." Cf. also Jombart, *Des Délits et des Peines,* p, 689, n. 110: "Une fois la monition faite sans résultat, la peine peut être infligée sans autre formalité"; Regatillo, *Institutiones Iuris Canonici* (2 vols., Santander: Sal Terrae, 1941-1942), II, p. 390, n. 1040: ". . . ipsa monitio cum comminatione poenae est processus"; Cloran, *Previews and Practical Cases,* pp. 221-222: "No special procedure is required in the infliction of this penalty, but an admonition or warning is essential."

[32] Cf. *Ius Canonicum,* VII, p. 367, n. 349V.

In so far as a temporary deprivation of the clerical garb is meant as punishment for just such transgressions from which there results a grave scandal that cannot be remedied in any other way, the delict contemplated by the Code as the fit object for this penalty would certainly come within the purview of canon 2222, § 1. The prerequisite element of scandal as postulated in canon 2300 is delineated in such broad terms (limited only by the fact that it cannot be removed in any other way) that one is forced to conclude that a temporary deprivation of the clerical garb is always an indeterminate penalty, and may have as its legitimate object the violation of any number of ecclesiastical laws, provided that the violation is accompanied with grave scandal which cannot be removed in any other way. For example, the cleric in question could give grave scandal by flouting one or the other of the clerical obligations listed in the common law.[33]

Many of these laws pertaining to the cleric's obligations as a cleric are simply stated in that particular section of the Code without being matched by any corresponding penal canon in the fifth book of the Code for the punishment of their transgression. Thus the violation of these canons would truly be the violation of an ecclesiastical law to which no sanction of any specific penalty is attached. For example, clerics are expressly forbidden to enter saloons apart from necessity or without a just cause approved by the ordinary.[34] Ordinarily the violation of this canon in a particular case by a particular cleric could not be punished as a delict (in the sense of canon 2195) unless a penalty were provided by particular legislation (e.g., synodal law). If, however, the violation of this canon was attended with notable scandal and particular gravity (e.g., because of the cleric's habitual public drunkenness), then it could be punished by the ordinary in virtue of canon 2222, § 1.[35]

---

[33] *CIC,* canons 124-144, lib. II, pars I, sect. I, tit. III.

[34] Canon 138: "Clerici ab iis omnibus quae statum suum dedecent, prorsus abstineant: . . . tabernas aliaque similia loca sine necessitate aut alia iusta causa ab Ordinario loci probata ne ingrediantur."

[35] Cf. Casey, *A Study of Canon 2222 § 1,* Catholic University of America Canon Law Studies, n. 290 (Washington, D. C.: Catholic University of America Press, 1949), p. 64.

The question arises, however, of just what penalty could be inflicted on the delinquent cleric in virtue of canon 2222, § 1, when the circumstances of notable scandal or of a particular gravity is verified as in the case supposed. The canon simply states that "some just penalty" can be inflicted. Casey asserts that the penalty thus inflicted would have to be a *ferendae sententiae* vindicative penalty (which a temporary deprivation of the clerical garb certainly is), but he goes on to say that the penalty could not be one of those to which the Code has attached a reserve clause which permits their infliction only in punishment of certain specified delicts. Among the excluded penalties he lists deposition, degradation, deprivation of the clerical garb (whether for a time or *in perpetuum*), infamy of law, and the penal deprivation of an irremovable office.[36]

The present writer feels disinclined to agree with this list in its entirety. While it is true that deposition,[37] degradation,[38] perpetual deprivation of the clerical garb,[39] infamy of law[40] and the penal deprivation of an irremovable office[41] are reserved as punishment for only certain specified crimes, there is no such reservation placed on the use of temporary deprivation of the clerical garb either explicitly or implicitly in the common law of the Code. Accordingly this penalty could be inflicted in virtue of the special faculty granted in canon 2222, namely when no other penalty would prove effective in removing the scandal.

Because of the severity of this penalty, however, canon 2222, § 1, is derogated somewhat in so far as a prior warning must be given, even though there is present the element of notable scandal or peculiar gravity which ordinarily would excuse the superior from the necessity of issuing a prior warning. In other words, in the case cited, the superior could avail himself of the special faculty granted in canon 2222, § 1, for the punishing of a cleric

---

[36] Cf. *op. cit.*, pp. 92-100.
[37] Canon 2303, § 3.
[38] Canon 2305, § 2.
[39] Canon 2304 taken with canon 2303, § 3.
[40] Canon 2293, § 2.
[41] Canon 2299, § 1.

who would cause grave scandal by his habitual public drunkenness, but he could not omit the prior warning if temporary deprivation of the cleric's garb is the only effective penalty which he can employ.[42]

Granted that the penalty in question can be inflicted for the transgression of non-penal laws, provided that a prior warning has been given and that it is the only way in which the scandal can be removed, there still remains the question of whether or not it can be inflicted immediately by way of extrajudicial precept when the delinquent fails to heed the warning given, or whether it must be inflicted by way of condemnatory sentence in a judicial trial. Certainly its infliction is not reserved to a collegiate tribunal of five judges, as is the case with a perpetual deprivation of the garb. This is evident from the fact that canon 1576, § 1, 2°, by its explicit mention of *perpetual* deprivation alone implicitly excludes *temporary* deprivation from such a restriction. The fact that it is similarly excluded from the necessity of being tried in a criminal trial before one judge is not so easily proved.

In his commentary on canon 2222, § 1, Casey maintains that the ordinary way in which penalties are to be inflicted in virtue of the special faculty granted there is that of a condemnatory sentence in a criminal trial, and that the infliction of these penalties by way of an extrajudicial precept is subject to rigid limitations.[43] Among the limitations which Casey cites is the limitation derived from the nature of the penalty to be imposed. If an extrajudicial precept is to be employed for the infliction of the penalty, then the penalty inflicted can only be one of those that are listed in canon 1933, § 4, viz., penal remedies and penances, excom-

---

[42] This conclusion seems justified from the fact that the Code in canon 2222, § 1, uses the word *"etiam"* to introduce the phrase which empowers the superior to dispense with a warning in the case of notable scandal or peculiar gravity. In other words, the giving of a prior warning is not entirely excluded even in regard to those penalties which do not require a prior warning by express provision of law. With those that do, however (as is the case with temporary deprivation of the clerical garb), the special faculty of canon 2222, § 1, is derogated to that extent; cf. Reg. 34, R. J. in VI°: "Generi per speciem derogatur."

[43] Cf. *A Study of Canon 2222, § 1*, pp. 80-89, 93-94.

munication, suspension, and interdict.[44] Accordingly, a temporary deprivation of the clerical garb, since it is not included in the enumeration of canon 1933, § 4, would demand a judicial trial for its infliction.

The present writer feels constrained to agree with Casey in his strict interpretation of this disputed canon. As Roberti himself (the chief proponent of the opposite opinion) admits, this strict interpretation is more in harmony with the penal laws of the Code.[45] Hence the writer must disagree with the opinion of the authors cited at the beginning of this section who maintain that the warning alone is sufficient, and that no other special procedure is necessary for the infliction of the penalty. The only exception which he would make to this ordinary norm of judicial procedure would attach to the case wherein a cleric persisted in giving grave scandal and his incorrigibility was truly notorious in fact. Then the legitimate superior of the delinquent cleric in question could inflict a temporary deprivation of the offender's garb extrajudicially in virtue of the pre-Code *processus e notorio.* This process will be explained in more detail in section 3 of the following article, when the same problem is treated with regard to the possibility of extrajudicially inflicting a *perpetual* deprivation of the clerical garb.

ARTICLE 2. PROCEDURE IN THE INFLICTION OF PERPETUAL DEPRIVATION OF THE GARB

Section 1. Prerequisites

Before an ordinary can proceed to punish a cleric with perpetual deprivation of his distinctive garb, there are certain prerequisites which must be observed. The cleric must first be deposed for one of the crimes which the Code of Canon Law expressly

---

[44] Cf. Casey, *op. cit.,* pp. 93-94; this limitation is deduced from Casey's belief that the enumeration of penalties in canon 1933, § 4, is complete and exclusive. For a discussion of the different interpretations given this canon, cf. pp. 104-118.

[45] Cf. *De Poenis in Genere,* p. 294, n. 259.

punishes with the penalty of deposition.[46] Secondly, it must be ascertained that the cleric has evinced no sign of repentance after deposition, but rather has continued to give scandal.[47] Thirdly, the cleric must have been admonished to desist from his evil ways and shown no response to the admonitions given him.[48]

All three of these prerequisite circumstances must be simultaneously present before the ordinary can proceed to inflict the penalty in question.[49] The last two of these three prerequisites, however, could really be considered as one, since ordinarily the fact of incorrigibility after deposition will be determined by the cleric's lack of response to the admonitions given him.[50] Concerning the warning to be given, the following is worthy of note. Although the delinquent may be given more than one opportunity to change his evil mode of living, one warning given in vain would constitute sufficient reason for the ordinary to start proceedings for the infliction of perpetual deprivation of the offender's garb.[51] All the remarks which were made in the preceding article with reference to the warning given before the infliction of a temporary deprivation of the clerical garb are applicable also to this warning as required before the infliction of a perpetual deprivation.

Concerning the consequent incorrigibility postulated for the

---

[46] Cf. canons 2304, § 1: "Si clericus depositus . . ." and 2303, § 3: "Poena depositionis infligi nequit, nisi in casibus iure expressis." Cf. also Findlay, *Deposition and Degradation,* p. 176.

[47] Cf. canon 2304, § 1: ". . . non det emendationis signa et praesertim si scandalum dare pergat . . ."; Findlay, *loc. cit.*

[48] Cf. canon 2304, § 1: ". . . monitusque non resipiscat . . ."; Findlay, *loc. cit.*

[49] Cf. Findlay, *loc. cit.;* Augustine, *Commentary,* VIII, 261; Sipos, *Enchiridion,* § 240, p. 948.

[50] Cf. Findlay, *loc. cit.*

[51] Cf. Berutti, *De Delictis et Poenis,* p. 234, n. 91: "Ut certo constet de rei obstinatione in delinquendo vel in vita publice immorigera et scandalosa, oportet ut Ordinarius antequam perpetuo eum privet iure deferendi habitum ecclesiasticum semel saltem, etsi forsan secreto, illum moneat"; Coronata, *Institutiones,* IV, p. 274, n. 1835. The use of the phrase *monitusque non resipiscat* without any qualifying numerical adverb in canon 2304, § 1, seems to bear out this opinion.

infliction of this penalty, the following question may be raised. Must the deposed cleric again commit a delict of the same specific gravity as that which warranted his deposition before he can be deprived perpetually of his right to wear the clerical garb, or would it suffice that the cleric have committed any one of the nine other delicts expressly punished by the Code with deposition? For example, would a cleric, once he has been deposed in accordance with canon 2320 for desecration of the Sacred Species, again have to desecrate the Sacred Species or would the fact that he commits, let us say, an abortion after deposition suffice to warrant his being perpetually deprived of his clerical garb? In the opinion of the writer, the committing of any one of the delicts expressly punished by the Code with deposition would suffice as a reason for the deposed cleric's ordinary to proceed further and to deprive him perpetually of his clerical garb.[52]

Indeed, it seems that the deposed cleric would not have to be a recidivist even in this generic sense of the term. Since canon 2304 states that the ordinary can inflict perpetual deprivation of the clerical garb on a deposed cleric if the latter shows no sign of amendment, and especially if he continues to give scandal and does not heed the admonitions given him, it appears that the penalty in question could be inflicted even for delicts of lesser gravity than those which warrant deposition, as long as the conditions as postulated in the canon are verified. The notions of scandal and incorrigibility are obviously present in delicts other than those punished with deposition. If the delict perpetrated after deposition be one that is of even graver character than those which warrant deposition as their penalty (e.g., the delicts which have degradation as their penalty from the express provision of the Code), obviously the correct procedure for the ordinary to follow is to pass over the infliction of perpetual deprivation of the clerical garb *qua talis,* and to proceed immediately to the infliction of the graver penalty of degradation, which contains perpetual deprivation of the garb as one of its constituent elements.[53]

---

[52] Cf. Findlay, *Deposition and Degradation,* p. 177.
[53] Canon 2305.

Section 2. The Necessity of Two Separate Trials

Since a prior deposition is always postulated, one may raise the question whether or not the criminal trial before five judges, as required by canon 1576, § 1, 2°, in all cases of deposition, could suffice for the infliction of perpetual deprivation of the deposed cleric's garb when the fact of continued incorrigibility even after the deposition is clearly evident. If so, the seeming unnecessary formalities of a second criminal trial before a collegiate tribunal would be obviated. This indeed seems to be the opinion of Coronata, for he states that no special manner of procedure or no special tribunal is required for the infliction of a perpetual deprivation of the garb, but that the ordinary can proceed by himself, provided he has given at least one warning to the delinquent cleric without result.[54]

Such an opinion is difficult to reconcile with the express law of the Code which reserves the infliction not only of deposition but also perpetual deprivation of the garb to a collegiate tribunal of five judges. Indeed, any contrary custom is expressly reprobated and any contrary privilege expressly revoked.[55] Because of the explicit language employed in this canon, Findlay felt constrained to label this opinion of Coronata's "manifestly erroneous."[56] Indeed Coronata simply asserts his opinion in a very positive fashion as though there were no room for doubt. He adduces no intrinsic argumentation from the Code itself, nor does he appeal to any extrinsic argumentation from authority. One might well invoke the principle: "*Quod gratis asseritur, gratis negatur.*"

A more cogent answer, however, derives from a consideration of just what matters would have to be treated in a criminal trial held for the infliction of perpetual deprivation of the garb. Such a trial would have to concern itself with the question of whether or not the deposed and incorrigible cleric had been given a warning

[54] Cf. *Institutiones,* IV, p. 274, n. 1835.

[55] Canon 1576, § 1: "Reprobata contraria consuetudine et revocata quolibet contrario privilegio . . . 2°. Causae vero quibus agitur de delictis quae depositionis, privationis perpetuae habitus ecclesiasticae . . . poenam importtant, reservantur tribunali quinque iudicum."

[56] Cf. *Deposition and Degradation,* p. 178, fn. 352; cf. also Vermeersch-Creusen, *Epitome,* III, p. 303, n. 497; Sipos, *Enchiridion,* § 240, p. 948.

to desist from his scandalous conduct, and with what results, whereas the trial held for the infliction of deposition would concern itself only with the question of whether or not one of the ten specific delicts punished by the Code with deposition had been perpetrated by the delinquent cleric. For the infliction of perpetual deprivation of the garb, moreover, it would have to be proved that the offender had manifested no signs of amendment *after* deposition but rather had continued to give scandal. Then and only then could the ordinary proceed to deprive the offender of his clerical garb *in perpetuum*. Consequently, the necessity of two separate trials can hardly be denied.[57]

Section 3. Controversy Concerning the Possibility of Inflicting Perpetual Deprivation of the Garb by Extrajudicial Precept

Of more practical importance, however, than the question of whether or not two distinct criminal trials are demanded by the law of the Code is the question of whether or not any criminal trial at all is required when the commission of the delict is certain, or when great harm would ensue to the good of souls because of the scandal which would continue to be given until a judicial sentence could be reached. If this question could be answered in the negative, then the opinion of Coronata could be sustained.[58]

In view of the explicit regulation laid down in the Code that "trials in connection with crimes which entail the penalties of deposition, perpetual deprivation of the clerical garb, or degradation, are reserved to a tribunal of five judges,"[59] one may wonder how anyone could maintain that the formality of a criminal trial for the infliction of these penalties could be dispensed with even in the particular circumstances delimited above. The answer lies

---

[57] Cf. Findlay, *Deposition and Degradation*, pp. 177-178; Blat, *Commentarium*, V, p. 186, n. 137.

[58] Coronata himself, however, with regard to the penalty of deposition, does not admit that this penalty could be inflicted by way of an extrajudicial particular precept substituted for the criminal trial demanded in canon 1576, § 1, 2°. Cf. *Institutiones*, III, 379-382; IV, 274.

[59] Canon 1576, § 1, 2°; translation from Woywod, *A Practical Commentary on the Code of Canon Law* (revised and enlarged edition, 2 vols., New York: Wagner, 1948), II, 232 (hereafter cited as *Commentary*).

in the interpretation which one makes of canon 1933, § 4. This canon reads as follows: "§ 1. Offenses which are subject to criminal procedure are public offenses . . . § 4. Penances, penal remedies, excommunication, suspension, and interdict can be inflicted also by way of precept without judicial procedure, provided the offense is certain."[60]

There are several schools of thought as to the interpretation of this latter paragraph. One of them holds that the list of penalties recounted therein is complete and exclusive: only the penalties there mentioned can be inflicted by way of extrajudicial precept, and these only when they have been established by precept.[61] Another opinion, while agreeing with the first that the enumeration of penalties in canon 1933, § 4, is complete and exclusive, maintains that these penalties can be inflicted by way of extrajudicial precept regardless of whether they were established by law or by precept.[62] A third interpretation asserts that not only the penalties listed in canon 1933, § 4, but also any other penalties which have been established by precept *ad instar legis* can be inflicted by way of extrajudicial precept.[63] Finally, a fourth opinion maintains that any penalty (regardless of whether it has been established by law or by precept) can be applied by way of extrajudicial precept, with the exception of those cases in which a judicial trial is absolutely required.[64]

Since perpetual deprivation of the clerical garb has been estab-

---

[60] Translation from Woywod, *Commentary,* II, 355.

[61] Cf., e.g., Noval, "De Ratione Corrigendi et Puniendi sive in Iudicio sive extra Iure Codicis I. C.," *Jus Pontificium,* II, fasc. 4 (Oct.-Dec., 1922), p. 156; Coronata, *Institutiones,* III, 380.

[62] According to Roberti, Cappello insinuates this opinion with some doubt in his *De Censuris,* n. 76; cf. Roberti, *De Poenis in Genere,* p. 295, n. 260. Coronata, however, correctly points out that the proponents of this second interpretation assume the fact of a complete and exclusive enumeration in canon 1933, § 4, whereas Cappello argues for a merely demonstrative enumeration in his article, "Irrogatio Poenae per Modum Praecepti extra Iudicium," *Periodica de Re Morali, Canonica, Liturgica,* XIX (1930), pp. 36*-38*; cf. Coronata, *Institutiones,* III, 380, fn. 2.

[63] Cf., e.g., Chelodi, *Ius Poenale,* n. 25; Vermeersch-Creusen, *Epitome,* III (6. ed., 1946), p. 247, n. 415.

[64] Cf. e.g., Roberti, *De Poenis in Genere,* p. 296, n. 262.

lished by the common law of the Code and is not enumerated in the list of penalties delineated in canon 1933, § 4, further discussion of the first three interpretations of that particular paragraph will be of little avail for an understanding of the point at hand. Those interpretations would certainly exclude the penalty in question from the number of those which can be inflicted by way of extrajudicial precept in lieu of a criminal trial when the peculiar circumstances already noted are present in a particular case.[65] It is with the fourth interpretation that one must be concerned. (While it is true that the protagonists of this opinion expressly except cases in which a judicial trial is absolutely required [e.g., cases of perpetual deprivation of the clerical garb in virtue of canon 1576, § 1, 2°] from those penalties which can be inflicted by way of extrajudicial precept, still the arguments which they adduce for their interpretation provide grounds for the formulation of what one might term a fifth school of thought, which would not even exempt these cases when a judicial trial would not serve any purpose or when the time necessary to reach a sentence in a judicial trial would militate against the good of souls.) The principal argument advanced by the members of this fourth school of thought in behalf of the opinion which they adopt is deduced from the almost universal practice in vogue before the Code (and indeed a very common practice even now in the Roman Congregations as well as in inferior ecclesiastical tribunals) of inflicting penalties other than those listed in canon 1933, § 4, by way of extrajudicial precept rather than by way of judicial trial.[66]

Coronata objects to this argument for the following reasons:

[65] For a more complete treatment of the reasons motivating the proponents of these first three schools to postulate what they do, and for the objections which may be brought against each of these opinions, the reader is referred to Roberti, *op. cit.*, pp. 294-296. The same material may also be found verbatim in an article on the subject written by the same author and published in the periodical, *Apollinaris*, IV (1931), 294-300.

[66] Cf. Roberti, *De Poenis in Genere*, pp. 294-297, where he appeals to this *de facto* accepted mode of inflicting extra-judicially penalties other than those enumerated in canon 1933, § 4, no less than four times while objecting to the other interpretations of that canon and in sustaining his own; idem, "Quaenam Poenae Applicari Possint per Modum Praecepti?" *Apollinaris*, IV (1931), 294-300.

Roberti cites no examples in verification of his assertion;[67] such a practice may reflect an abuse rather than a legitimate use of power;[68] even if it were proved legitimate, perhaps it could be explained by special grants in the Code, such as the ones contained in canons 188; 454, § 5; 471, § 3; 595, § 3; 646; 653; 970; 2222, § 2; etc.;[69] moreover, regarding the claim that such was the almost universal practice prior to the promulgation of the Code, it must be remembered that the Code has abrogated such penal customs which are contrary to it and are not given reexpression in it, as Roberti himself acknowledges.[70]

All of these objections offered by Coronata seem to be justified. Indeed, the conclusion as drawn from this argument by Roberti himself, namely that one cannot put lightly aside such a common practice of many ecclesiastical curias when that practice is modeled on the *stylus* of the Roman Curia itself, is open to objection. Roberti cites canon 20 of the Code as the basis for this last statement.[71] Canon 20, however, deals with the establishment of a suppletory norm, and not with the extension of laws which are already in existence.[72] Moreover, recourse to the principles stated there (among them being the style and practice of the Roman Curia) is expressly forbidden in whatever application needs to be made with reference to penalties.[73]

Cappello, in presenting his version of this fourth interpretation of canon 1933, § 4, goes one step further than Roberti, since he does not even except those penalties for which a judicial process is absolutely required.[74] Indeed, he explicitly refers his reader to

[67] Cf. *Institutiones,* III, 380, fn. 8; cf. also Esswein, *The Extrajudicial Coercive Powers of Ecclesiastical Superiors,* Catholic University of America Canon Law Studies, n. 127 (Washington, D. C.: Catholic University of America Press, 1941), p. 113.

[68] Cf. Coronata, *op. cit.,* III, 380; Esswein, *loc. cit.*

[69] Cf. Coronata, *loc. cit.*

[70] Cf. Coronata, *op. cit.,* III, 380-381; Esswein, *loc. cit.;* Roberti, *De Delictis in Genere,* pp. 77-78, n. 55; cf. also canon 6, 5°.

[71] Cf. *De Poenis in Genere,* p. 297.

[72] Cf. Coronata, *Ius Publicum Ecclesiasticum,* p. 272, n. 192.

[73] Canon 20.

[74] Cf. Cappello, "Irrogatio Poenae per Modum Praecepti extra Iudicium," *Periodica de Re Morali, Canonica, Liturgica,* XIX (1930), pp. 36*-38*.

the vindicative penalties enumerated in canon 2298 as examples of what other penalties he has in mind without making any distinction as to those which absolutely require a judicial process (e.g., perpetual deprivation of the garb in virtue of canon 1576, § 1, 2°). Thus Cappello actually constitutes a fifth interpretation of the disputed canon, notwithstanding the fact that Roberti claims him as a colleague in his school of thought.[75]

Cappello presents the following argument in support of his contention. First, as a *conditio sine qua non,* he requires that the delict be certain not only as to the material fact, but also as to its moral imputability (i.e., that the delict be a transgression of a penal law which is certainly known in order that it might constitute a true delict according to the norm of canon 2195). If this condition be verified, then the penalty can be inflicted by way of precept extrajudicially without the necessity of a judicial procedure, whenever the lapse of the period of time which is necessarily consumed in the drawing up of a criminal trial would occasion harm for the good of souls because of the scandal which would thus be protracted until a judicial sentence could be executed. The reason given is deduced from the principle that the good of souls is to be religiously safeguarded and procured.

While admitting that this is merely a persuasive argument, Cappello points out that this principle is clearly and expressly approved by the Code itself with regard to the infliction of suspension *ex informata conscientia* in canon 2191, § 3, 3°.[76] Thus the way is opened for the infliction of all penalties by way of extrajudicial precept regardless of whether or not a judicial trial is absolutely required by the Code for their infliction. Roberti himself, while he interprets canon 1933, § 4, in a very broad fashion, does not agree with Cappello on this point, for, as he points out, it is doubtful whether the singular manner of proceeding in the infliction of suspension *ex informata conscientia* can be applied analogically to the ordinary judicial process.[77] Coronata, moreover,

[75] Cf. Roberti, *De Poenis in Genere,* p. 296.

[76] Cf. Cappello, *loc. cit.*

[77] Cf. Roberti, *op. cit.,* p. 298; cf. also Coronata, *Institutiones,* III, 381, fn. 4, where he states that this would constitute a violation of canon 2219, § 3: "Non licet poenam . . . de casu ad casum producere, quamvis par adsit ratio, imo gravior. . . ."

though he admits the validity of the application of the principle "*Salus animarum suprema lex*," with reference to the establishment of law, denies any like validity when there is question of the interpretation of a law already established, especially when the law being interpreted is a penal law in which any extension in interpretation must be avoided.[78]

Though Cappello does not employ it, another argument for the validity of an ordinary's action by way of extrajudicial precept rather than by judicial trial in inflicting penalties which absolutely require a judicial process (e.g., perpetual deprivation of the garb) could derive from the fact that excommunication can be so inflicted.[79] Since excommunication is by its very nature and because of its effects the most severe penalty that can be inflicted on a delinquent,[80] *a fortiori* the lesser penalty of perpetual deprivation of the garb can be inflicted extrajudicially when the delict is certain.

By way of answer to this argument, some remarks of Findlay are in order. Comparing the vindicative penalty of degradation with the medicinal penalty of excommunication, he has the following comments to make: ". . . whereas degradation remains the most severe vindictive penalty with which a cleric as cleric can be punished, there is still the more severe medicinal penalty of excommunication with which the degraded cleric as a member of the Church may be punished . . . from another viewpoint it could be maintained that degradation is even a more severe penalty than excommunication. The latter is always a censure, and never a vindictive penalty (canon 2255, § 2). In consequence it must be absolved as soon as the delinquent with proper dispositions seeks absolution (canon 2241, § 1). Degradation on the other hand is never a censure but always a vindictive penalty (canon 2298, 12°). No matter how repentant the degraded cleric may become, he acquires thereby no right to have his penalty removed (canon 2286)."[81] The same argument can just as readily be ad-

[78] *Op. cit.*, p. 381; canons 20 and 2219.

[79] Canon 1933, § 4: ". . . excommunicatio . . . dummodo delictum certum sit, infligi (potest) etiam per modum praecepti extra iudicium."

[80] Cf. canons 2241, § 2; 2257-2267.

[81] Cf. Findlay, *Deposition and Degradation*, p. 219.

duced, *mutatis mutandis,* with regard to the relative severity which exists between the vindicative penalty of perpetual deprivation of the clerical garb and the medicinal penalty of excommunication.

Another argument, however, which Cappello *does* advance for the foregoing of all judicial procedure in favor of the use of extra-judicial precept when the commission of the delict is notorious is that which derives from the very nature of a criminal trial, the whole purpose of which (namely, the detection of a crime and its author) would be rendered superfluous under the circumstances here postulated.[82] While Cappello does not refer to it, a decree of the Sacred Roman Rota in the year 1910 corroborating this argument could here be pointed out. The case in which this decree was handed down concerned the propriety of a bishop's action who had suspended his vicar forane and deprived him of his office without judicial procedure because of the latter's contumacious refusal to abide by the bishop's decision settling a conflict of rights over the holding of a Corpus Christi procession. The conflict had arisen between the Dominican Fathers and the cleric in question. Indeed the vicar forane had appealed to the civil authority as well as to various ecclesiastical superiors. The Rota decided that in notorious crimes such as this a judicial trial was unnecessary. The reason given was: ". . . iudicium inservit ad detegendum crimen et criminis auctorem, quare iudicialis processus est fere supervacaneus, quando reus nullo potest argumento sese excusare ab impacto crimine, cum evidentia adversus eum clamet."[83]

The logic of this reasoning by the Rota cannot be denied.

As to the adoption by inferior ecclesiastical tribunals of the practice therein exemplified, however, the following may be objected. First of all, the penalties concerned in this decree of the Rota were suspension and deprivation of the office of vicar forane. Since suspension is one of the penalties specifically mentioned in the Code as being subject to infliction by way of extra-judicial precept when the delict is certain, and since the Code

[82] Cf. Cappello, *loc. cit.*

[83] Cf. *Sacrae Romanae Rotae Decisiones seu Sententiae* (*ab anno 1909*) (Romae: Typis Polyglottis Vaticanis, 1912-), II (1910), decis. XX, p. 196.

expressly states that the vicar forane is removable from his office *ad nutum episcopi* (as he was even as early as the 16th century), it hardly seems valid to cite the infliction of these penalties by way of extrajudicial precept as a precedent for the infliction of other penalties in the same manner when the same circumstances obtain.[84]

Moreover, this decree was given in 1910, eight years before the enactment of the Code. Since the Code expressly demands a criminal trial before a collegiate tribunal of five judges for the infliction of perpetual deprivation of the clerical garb, it is difficult to see how the practice of employing an extrajudicial precept for the infliction of at least this particular penalty (even when the case is notorious) could still be sustained after 1918. The reason for this statement is the fact that the Code has abrogated all prior customs which are contrary to the prescriptions set down in the Code and expressly reprobated by it. These two conditions of contrariety to the prescriptions of the Code and the express reprobation enacted by the Code are verified in the custom of inflicting perpetual deprivation of the clerical garb by way of extrajudicial precept rather than by way of condemnatory sentence in a collegiate tribunal. Accordingly the Code has abrogated this custom and does not allow it to revive.[85]

These objections, however, are only partially valid. While it is true that the infliction of suspension and deprivation of the office of vicar forane by way of extrajudicial precept should not be looked to as a precedent for the infliction of other penalties in the same manner, one cannot as easily dismiss the general conclusion drawn from this particular case, viz., that a judicial trial of its very nature is superfluous in the case of any notorious delict,

[84] Canons 1933, § 4, and 446, § 2; cf. Ferraris, *Prompta Bibliotheca*, VII, 568, s.v., "vicarius foraneus," n. 5.

[85] Cf. canons 5: "Vigentes in praesens contra horum statuta canonum consuetudines sive universales sive particulares, si quidem ipsis canonibus expresse reprobentur, tanquam iuris corruptelae corrigantur, licet sint immemorabiles, neve sinantur in posterum reviviscere; . . ." and 1576, § 1: "Reprobata contraria consuetudine et revocato quolibet contrario privilegio: . . . 2°. Causae vero quibus agitur de delictis quae depositionis, privationis perpetuae habitus ecclesiastici, vel degradationis poenam important, reserventur tribunali quinque iudicum"; Coronata, *Institutiones* I, 8; III, 380-381.

no matter what be the nature of the penalty that is to be inflicted. With regard to the second objection—that the Code has abrogated the custom of inflicting perpetual deprivation of the clerical garb by way of an extrajudicial precept rather than by way of a judicial process—one must consider whether the Code has abrogated this custom under any and all circumstances, or whether it still allows this custom under certain specified circumstances which constitute, as it were, an exception to the ordinary manner of procedure.

In the opinion of the writer, the infliction of a perpetual deprivation of the clerical garb by way of extrajudicial precept (while by no means the ordinary procedure) can still be sustained when the commission of the delict is notorious. Ordinarily it is true that the infliction of this penalty is reserved to a collegiate tribunal of five judges, in virtue of the express provision of canon 1576, § 1, 2°. Allowance for the infliction of this penalty by way of the extraordinary method of an extrajudicial precept, however, is implicit in the Code when the delict is notorious. This must be admitted; otherwise there could be no reconciliation of apparent contradictions in the Code.

The Code, for example, demands that this penalty be inflicted by way of a condemnatory sentence issued by a collegiate tribunal of five members. In other words, the Code demands a criminal trial for the infliction of this penalty. Now, the purpose of a criminal trial is the same as that of trials in general, namely, the discussion and definition of facts which need to be proved.[86] In a later canon, however, the Code explicitly states that notorious facts (*a pari* notorious delicts, especially since express mention is made of canon 2197) do not need to be proved.[87] Implicit in canon 1747, therefore, is the established fact that in the case of notorious delicts no criminal trial is necessary for the infliction of the called for penalties. What procedure then is to be followed for the infliction of suitable penalties in punishment of such notorious delicts?

---

[86] Canon 1552, § 1.

[87] Canon 1747: "Non indigent probatione: 1°. Facta notoria ad normam can. 2197, nn. 2, 3; . . ."

Since the Code implicitly rules out the ordinary criminal trial, it also *implicitly* retains the *processus e notorio* of the pre-Code law, in which there was not required any *citatio,* any *libellus supplex,* or any *litis contestatio,* and against which there was not any invoking of an appeal, as is evident from various texts found in Decretal Law, and from the various commentaries on these texts by the Decretalists and subsequent pre-Code authors.[88] And since the Code does not *explicitly* mention this process, one is compelled to evaluate it wholly from the authority of the pre-Code law, i.e., from the interpretation given this process by approved authors.[89] This is made even more necessary by the fact that more recent authors say little or nothing about this process, outside of mentioning the fact that it still exists.

Moreover, since the Code *has implicitly retained* this process, by that very fact it bids one to reject the opinion of those pre-Code authors who, while they admitted the existence of the *processus e notorio,* still taught that in practice it was more expedient[90] or even necessary[91] that the judge proceed *ad normam iuris,* even in the case of delicts notorious with a factual notoriety. If the Code recognizes such a process through its implicit retention of it, then certainly it must envision the use of that process when in a given case there concur all the circumstances that justifiably demand such an extraordinary procedure.[92]

A few cautions are warranted, however, with regard to the use of this process. First of all, it must be clearly evident that the delict is actually notorious, for, if it is not, the whole *processus e notorio* would lack foundation. Consequently, at least two witnesses must testify concerning not only the delict itself, but also the notoriety of the delict, namely concerning the fact that it was

[88] Cf. Dougherty, *De Inquisitione Speciali,* Catholic University of America Canon Law Studies, n. 213 (Washington, D. C.: Catholic University of America Press, 1945), pp. 111, fns. 28 and 29; 112, 113.

[89] Canon 6, 2°; cf. Dougherty, *op. cit.,* p. 112.

[90] Cf. Schmalzgrueber, *Ius Ecclesiasticum Universum,* lib. V, tit. I, n. 16; Reiffenstuel, *Ius Canonicum Universum,* lib. V, tit. I, n. 266.

[91] Cf. Lega, *Praelectiones in Textum Iuris Canonici, De Iudiciis Ecclesiasticis* (4 vols., Romae, 1896-1901), IV, pp. 176-177, n. 121.

[92] Cf. Dougherty, *op. cit.,* pp. 112, 113.

perpetrated in the presence of a multitude who were actually watching.[93]

Since the Code explicitly states that for its object a criminal trial looks to a public delict,[94] the necessity of clearly distinguishing between a delict that is merely public and one that is moreover notorious is immediately evident. As Dougherty so well says, if the ordinary mistakenly considers a delict notorious which in reality is merely public, he works a grave injustice on the delinquent by taking away from him the possibility of proving his innocence in a judicial trial. Conversely, if he should mistake a notorious delict for one that is merely public, he works an injustice on the tribunal by imposing on it a superfluous burden of proving what is already proved.[95]

Canon 1747, 1° lists both species of notorious delicts (i.e., the ones notorious in law as well as the ones notorious in fact) as not needing to be proved. Since, by its very definition, a delict that is notorious in law is one which has already become a *res iudicata* through the sentence of a competent judge, or one which the delinquent has already confessed in trial according to the norm of canon 1750,[96] there is no need to treat of such notorious delicts here.

It is with a delict that is notorious in fact that one must be concerned, lest it be confused with a merely public delict, for thus there could result a wrong decision of whether or not a criminal trial is necessary for the infliction of the penalty. A delict which is notorious in fact is defined as one which is publicly known and committed in such circumstances that it cannot any longer be hidden or excused by means of any protection through law.[97] A public delict is defined as one which has already been divulged, or as one which has been committed under such circumstances that one prudently can and must judge that it will easily be divulged.[98]

There exist two opinions on just what is necessary to constitute

---

[93] Cf. Schmalzgrueber, *ibid.*, n. 16; Reiffenstuel, *ibid.*, n. 264.

[94] Canon 1933, § 1.

[95] Cf. Dougherty, *op. cit.*, p. 70.

[96] Canon 2197, 2°.

[97] Canon 2197, 3°.

[98] Canon 2197, 1°.

a delict that is notorious with a factual notoriety.[99] One opinion holds that "notorious with the notoriety of fact," connotes simply a species of the genus "public." For those who hold this opinion the delict must have already been divulged and to this divulgation there must in addition have acceded the two specific notions of indivertibleness and inexcusableness. In other words, the phrase *"publice notum"* of canon 2197, 3°, is equivalent to the definition of *"publicum"* as given in canon 2197, 1°.[100]

The second opinion, on the other hand, holds that this phrase *"publice notum"* of canon 2197, 3°, while on occasion (*per accidens*) it may be equivalent to the definition of *"publicum"* as given in canon 2197, 1°, still is not necessarily restricted to that interpretation. According to the proponents of this opinion, for the essence of a delict notorious with the notoriety of fact it suffices that there be *"notitia publica,"* which can derive not only from an actual divulgation or the imminent threat of divulgation, which alike constitute publicity for a delict, but also from other circumstances which give evidence to the existence of the delict in any public manner. Examples would be the detection of the delinquent *in actu flagranti* by a witness *omni exceptione maior* (e.g., the delinquent's superior) or the recording of the delict in some public document which is subject to the inspection of many people (even though *de facto* such a document be seldom if ever inspected).[101]

Inasmuch as there is question of a penal matter, the first opinion, namely that the phrase *"publice notum"* of canon 2197, 3°, is equivalent to the definition of *"publicum"* as given in canon 2197, 1°, will have to be followed, since it offers the milder interpretation the while it exists as a truly probable doctrine.[102] One cannot say, however, that *either* form of divulgation mentioned in canon 2197, 1° (i.e., actual or probable) will suffice to constitute the element of publicity postulated for any delict if it is to be regarded as notorious with the notoriety of fact. Only actual divulgation can satisfy that requirement. In other words, before

[99] For authors on both sides, cf. Dougherty, *op. cit.*, pp. 71-72, fns. 5 and 6.
[100] Cf. Dougherty, *op. cit.*, pp. 71-72.
[101] Cf. Dougherty, *op. cit.*, pp. 72-73.
[102] Cf. canons 19; 2219, § 1; Dougherty, *op. cit.*, pp. 72-75.

one can have a delict which is notorious with the notoriety of fact, it is necessary that the perpetration of the act of the delict itself and the imputability of the act as a delict, neither of which can any longer be hidden or excused by means of any legal device, be perceived simultaneously by a large number of bystanders.[103]

The reason for this limitation is twofold. First, that is the interpretation which was constantly and unanimously given in the pre-Code law. Before a delict was deemed notorious with the notoriety of fact in the pre-Code law, the delict had to be perpetrated before a large number of onlookers who perceived the inexcusable culpability of the delinquent at the same time that they perceived his performance of the delictual act itself.[104] Secondly, it is impossible to correlate the phrase *"publice notum"* of canon 2197, 3°, with the phrase *"divulgatum iri"* of canon 2197, 1°. While it is easy enough to admit that "publicly known" signifies the same thing as "already divulged," it is just as easy to see that what "will be divulged" is not yet "publicly known."[105]

The practical conclusion of this distinction is evident. If there be perpetrated a delict which is manifestly inexcusable in its moral imputability and evidently unchallengeable in its factual existence, but before only two or three witneses (even though they later relate the fact to many others), it can be punished only after a formal trial has been conducted according to the norms laid down in the fourth book of the Code. In such cases it would not be permissible to proceed *"e notorio."*

Another precaution must be attended to before an ordinary can utilize the *processus e notorio* for the infliction of perpetual deprivation of the garb. This final precaution is based on the triple division which commentators on the pre-Code law made with regard to factual notoriety. They distinguished notoriety of fact *actu transeuntis, actu manentis,* and *actu interpolati.*[106]

Notoriety of fact *actu transeuntis* occurred when a notorious

---

[103] Cf. Dougherty, *op. cit.,* p. 75.

[104] Cf. Dougherty, *op. cit.,* p. 74, fn. 12.

[105] Cf. Dougherty, *op. cit.,* pp. 75-76.

[106] Cf. *Decretum Gratiani emendatum et notationibus illustratum una cum glossis* (Romae, 1582), *Gl. Ord.,* ad c. 15, C. II, q. 1, s.v. *"manifesta";* Durandus, *Speculum Iuris,* lib. III, p. 50.

delict which had been committed once, or at most twice, in the past had later ceased to exist even in its effects.[107] Notoriety of fact *actu manentis* was deemed to occur when a notorious delict which had been committed in the past still persevered as to its effects up into the present, so that its perpetration was patent to all not once only but often.[108] Notoriety of fact *actu interpolati* was verified when a delict had been committed notoriously in the past and then was repeated a number of times intermittently, but without enduring effects.[109]

Only the second type mentioned, notoriety of fact *actu manentis,* needed no proof according to the interpretation given in the pre-Code law. The other two species still had to be proved in trial, although it was admitted that it was easier to prove them than the ordinary public delicts.[110] Since it has already been pointed out that the norms for interpreting the *processus e notorio* as it exists today must be taken from the norms given in the interpretation of the same process in the pre-Code law by approved authors, it is evident that the same restriction must be observed today. In other words, only a delict which was notorious in fact at the time of its commission and still endures as to its effects, so that its perpetration is often patent to a multitude of people, can be made the object of a *processus e notorio.*[111]

Applying the foregoing principles and limitations to the particular penalty of perpetual deprivation of the clerical garb, one may set down the following. Only under the following conditions may a deposed cleric be deprived perpetually of his right to wear the clerical garb by way of extrajudicial precept: 1.) The *objective* fact that the cleric has been justly deposed and has nevertheless remained incorrigible, paying no heed to the admonitions given him, must be already known by a great number of people; 2.) the *subjective* fact that the delinquent who continues to act thus is doing so in bad faith must also be apparent to the same people,

---

[107] Cf. Durandus, *loc. cit.;* Schmalzgrueber, *Ius Ecclesiasticum Universum,* lib. V, tit, I, n. 2.

[108] Cf. Durandus, *loc. cit.;* Schmalzgrueber, *loc. cit.*

[109] Cf. Durandus, *loc. cit.;* Schmalzgrueber, *loc. cit.*

[110] Cf. *Gl. Ord.,* ad c. 15, C. II, q. 1, s.v. "*manifesta.*"

[111] Cf. Dougherty, *op. cit.,* p. 78.

and 3.) at least two witnesses must have testified that these first two conditions are really verified and that the evil effects of such obdurate incorrigibility still endure up to the time when the penalty is to be inflicted. Otherwise, a perpetual deprivation of the clerical garb can be inflicted only by way of a condemnatory sentence passed in a criminal trial by a collegiate tribunal of five judges. Thus it is evident that the statement of Coronata that no judicial process is necessary for the infliction of this penalty can be admitted only in conjunction with the stringent limitations just listed. Similarly, the broad interpretation given to canon 1933, § 4, by Cappello seems capable of acceptance when the case in question is a truly notorious one.

Section 4. Infliction of Perpetual Deprivation of the Clerical Garb by Condemnatory Sentence in a Criminal Trial (the Ordinary Procedure)

The ordinary way for the inflicting of a perpetual deprivation of the clerical garb is to be effected by means of a condemnatory sentence handed down by a collegiate tribunal of five judges.[112] If the sentence were issued by a collegiate tribunal composed of less than five judges, the sentence would be vitiated with an incurable nullity.[113] This collegiate tribunal may be set up not only by the ordinary of the delinquent, but also by the ordinary of the place where the delict was committed. With regard to the penalty in question, this would mean that not only the ordinary who deposed a delinquent cleric, but also any other ordinary into whose territory the deposed cleric had come after deposition and where he was continuing to give scandal and refusing to amend, could institute proceedings against him.[114]

The associate judges of this collegiate tribunal ordinarily will be selected from the ranks of the synodal or pro-synodal judges *per turnum,* unless the ordinary for reasons of prudence deviates from this rule by selecting judges other than synodal or pro-synodal, or by appointing the synodal or pro-synodal judges out of

---

[112] Canon 1576, § 1, 2°.

[113] Canon 1892, 1°.

[114] Canons 1561; 1566.

rotation.[115] According to a declaration of the Commission for the Authentic Interpretation of the Code, not only the ordinary, but also the *officialis* who has been appointed by the ordinary according to canon 1573, §§ 1 and 2, with ordinary power to judge and without any reservation of cases, may set up this collegiate tribunal by calling in rotation the synodal or pro-synodal judges nominated according to canon 1574, unless the ordinary rules otherwise in a particular case.[116]

While the ordinary himself may preside over the tribunal in person, it is highly recommended that he forego the use of this right, since the matter involves a criminal trial.[117] Rather, the *officialis* or *vice-officialis* should act as the presiding judge, and it is his duty to direct the process and to decide those things which are necessary for the administration of justice in a given case.[118] No other requirement is necessary in these judges than that they be priests of good reputation who are well versed in canon law.[119] One of the four associate judges should be appointed by the presiding judge as the *ponens* or referee. It will be his duty to report on the case in the meeting of the judges and to commit the sentence to writing.[120]

The day and the hour when the five judges are to meet to discuss the case will be appointed by the presiding judge, and ordinarily this meeting will be held in the court room, unless the peculiar nature of the case makes another place preferable. At the meeting each judge should have prepared in writing his own conclusions on the merits of the case together with the reasons from fact and law which prompted such conclusions. All of these conclusions are to be added to the acts of the case and are to be kept secret. Reading of the conclusions should be made first by that judge who is acting as the referee; the others follow in the order of precedence.

---

[115] Canon 1576, § 3; Woywod, *Commentary*, II, 233.

[116] 28 iul. 1932—*AAS*, XXIV (1932), 314; Bouscaren, *The Canon Law Digest*, I, 742.

[117] Canon 1578.

[118] Canon 1577, § 2.

[119] Canons 1573, § 4; 1574, § 1.

[120] Canons 1584; 1872.

Finally, there should be a moderate discussion of the case under the direction of the presiding judge, mainly to determine how the decisive part of the sentence will read. During the course of the discussion each judge is free to abandon his original conclusions on the case. If, however, the judges cannot or do not wish to reach an agreement on the sentence in this first discussion, the decision may be postponed till another meeting, but they may not adjourn for more than a week.[121]

How the members of the collegiate tribunal come to the final sentence is not explicitly stated in the Code. There can be no doubt, however, that it is to be done by voting.[122] Unanimity of opinion is not necessary for the passing of the sentence. All that is required is a majority opinion, and the dissenting judge or judges must accede to and sign the majority decision.[123]

The *ponens* should make sure that the decisive part of the sentence contains the reasons both in law and in fact on which the decision is founded. These reasons should be drawn from the considerations which each judge adduced in the discussion, unless a plurality in the tribunal has agreed on and determined which motives should be given in the sentence.[124] Each judge must sign the sentence. If signatures were subscribed only by the presiding judge and the notary of the court, the sentence would be invalid in accordance with a declaration of the Commission for the Authentic Interpretation of the Code.[125]

When a plea of suspicion is entered against the entire tribunal or the majority of its members, although their competence in the case is admitted, the person who delegated the tribunal shall decide whether the objection is to be sustained. If the exception of

[121] Canon 1871.

[122] Cf. Woywood, *Commentary,* II, 331; canon 101 and 1873.

[123] Cf. Jombart, *Des Délits et des Peines,* p. 692, n. 1119; Vermeersch-Creusen, *Epitome, III,* p. 305, n. 499, 3°; Wernz, *Ius Decretalium,* VI, p. 136, n. 128; Berutti, *De Delictis et Poenis,* p. 236, n. 92, III; Findlay, *Deposition and Degradation,* p. 241; Lemieux, *The Sentence in Ecclesiastical Procedure,* Catholic University of America Canon Law Studies, n. 87 (Washington, D. C.: Catholic University of America, 1934), p. 86; canon 1577, § 1.

[124] Canon 1873, § 2.

[125] 14 iul. 1922—*AAS,* XIV (1922), 529; Bouscaren, *The Canon Law Digest,* I, 758; canons 1874, § 5; 1894, 3°.

suspicion is entered against only one or two particular members of the tribunal (even though that one member be the presiding judge), the other members of the tribunal will rule on the objection. If the exception be lodged against the *officialis,* the bishop will decide.[126] If the exception be brought against any other official of the court, the presiding judge will rule whether or not the objection can be sustained.[127] Whichever judges are declared suspect must be changed; if all five are so declared, then the whole tribunal must be changed. In this latter supposition, however, the case still remains in the same court. It is the duty of the ordinary to substitute in their place other judges who are immune from suspicion.[128]

As for the delict itself which is the object of this criminal trial, it must be remembered that if the incorrigibility and scandal after deposition is only occult, it cannot be punished in a criminal trial.[129] The fact that the deposed cleric has continued incorrigible must already have been divulged or at least connote the threat of easily becoming divulged.[130] Even if the fact of incorrigibility be certain or notorious in fact (with the exception of notoriety in fact *actu manentis*), the criminal trial must still be instituted, although in these cases the delict is easier to prove and no special inquisition needs to be employed beforehand.[131]

There is no need here to discuss at further length the criminal trial held for the infliction of this penalty. It is sufficient to point out that the general norms laid down in the Code for the conducting of all criminal trials must be observed in the conducting of this particular trial.[132]

Two points in particular, however, should be stressed. First, the collegiate tribunal may not suspend the execution of the sen-

---

[126] Canon 1614, § 1.

[127] Canon 1614, §§ 1, 3.

[128] Canon 1615.

[129] Canon 1933, § 1: "Delicta quae cadunt sub criminali iudicio sunt delicta publica."

[130] Canon 2197, 1°.

[131] Canon 1939, § 1; cf. Dougherty, *De Inquisitione Speciali,* pp. 78, 111-113.

[132] Cf. canons 1933-1959 incl., liber IV, pars prima, sectio secunda, tit. XIX, *CIC.*

tence once it has reached its decision. This power is indeed given to the judge by the common law of the Code, but only with reference to cases in which the delinquent has failed for the first time after a laudable life. Moreover, this discretionary power even with regard to first offenses is limited to cases in which there is no urgent reason for the repairing of scandal.[133] As is evident from the discussion of the prerequisites necessary before this penalty can be inflicted, neither condition required by the Code for the legitimate use of this discretionary power is present in the case under consideration.

Secondly, there seems to be no reason for the use of another discretionary power granted by the Code, namely, the substitution of a judicial rebuke for the criminal trial, if the delinquent cleric when questioned confesses his offense. The procedural law of the Code does allow an ordinary to substitute a judicial rebuke for the criminal trial in the contingency pointed out, but the same law also states that the judicial rebuke should not be substituted for the criminal trial when the ordinary deems it not sufficient for the reparation of scandal and the restoration of justice.[134] Again in virtue of the prerequisites which are required by the Code before perpetual deprivation of the clerical garb can be inflicted, it is difficult to see how the ordinary could come to any decision other than that the criminal trial is necessary for the reparation of the scandal given by the delinquent cleric and for the restoration of justice.

ARTICLE 3. APPEAL FROM THE SENTENCE

As has already been pointed out in the preceding article, there can be no question of an appeal when deprivation of the clerical garb has been inflicted extrajudicially in a *processus e notorio.* Outside of this extraordinary case, however, deprivation of the clerical garb, like any other vindicative penalty, can be appealed *in suspensivo.*[135] This appeal suspends the infliction of the penalty and leaves it to the court of second instance to conform to, to remit,

[133] Canon 2288.

[134] Canons 1947 and 1948, 3°.

[135] Canon 2287.

or to modify the sentence of the first tribunal which handled the case.

The appeal against the sentence of temporary or perpetual deprivation of the clerical garb given by the court of a suffragan bishop is carried to the metropolitan court. If the sentence is handed down in the first instance by the metropolitan court, then the appeal is taken to the court of that local ordinary whom the metropolitan, with the approval of the Holy See, has selected once and for all as representing his court of appeal. In virtue of the prescription set down in canon 285, archbishops who have no suffragans, and ordinaries (including prelates and abbots *nullius*) who are immediately subject to the Holy See, must choose a neighboring metropolitan with whom they will convene in council or synod. The court of this same metropolitan serves as their court of appeal.[136] In the case of exempt religious so punished, the appeal will be taken to the superior-general from a sentence handed down in the court of the provincial; to the abbot-president of a monastic congregation from the court of the local abbot.[137]

In all cases of appeal, the court of second instance must be established in the same fashion as the court of first instance. Accordingly, the court of appeal for a case of temporary deprivation of the clerical garb will consist of one judge; the court of appeal for a case involving perpetual deprivation of the garb will consist of a collegiate body of five judges.[138] In addition, the defrocked cleric may at any stage whatsoever of the procedure submit his case to the Holy See or lodge it there even in the first place.[139]

---

[136] Canon 1594, §§ 1-3.
[137] Canon 1594, § 4.
[138] Canon 1596.
[139] Canon 1569.

CHAPTER VI

Cessation of the Penalty

ARTICLE 1. CESSATION OF TEMPORARY DEPRIVATION OF THE CLERICAL GARB

Of its very nature, temporary deprivation of the clerical garb is inflicted upon a delinquent and incorrigible cleric with a view to its subsequent cessation after the lapse of a certain period of time deemed of sufficient duration for the expiation of the scandal and incorrigibility which warranted the infliction of so grave a penalty.[1] The *terminus ad quem* of this period of time may be specified or unspecified at the moment of the penalty's infliction, since this penalty can be inflicted for a definite period of time (e.g., several months or years) or even for some indefinite period (e.g., *ad beneplacitum Superioris*).[2] If the penalty has been inflicted for a definite period of time, then naturally it ceases once the period of time which was specified at the moment of its infliction has elapsed.[3]

If, on the other hand, at the moment of the penalty's infliction no definite period of time had been established as sufficient for the expiation of the delict, i.e., if the penalty had been inflicted *ad beneplacitum Superioris,* then any one of several factors could effect an *ipso facto* resulting termination of the penalty. The superior who inflicts this penalty *ad beneplacitum* can do so only in virtue of the jurisdiction which he has by reason of the office in relation to the delinquent. Consequently, on the part of the superior inflicting the penalty, one must take into consideration the various ways in which his jurisdiction could cease with a consequent automatic cessation of the penalty inflicted by him in virtue of that jurisdiction. Jurisdiction can be lost in any number

[1] Canon 2300: ". . . potest *interim* privari iure deferendi habitum ecclesiasticum; quae privatio, *dum perdurat,* . . ."

[2] Cf. Berutti, *De Delictis et Poenis,* p. 232, n. 89, 9°.

[3] Canon 2289: "Poena vindicativa finitur eius expiatione vel. . . ."

of ways: by express or tacit resignation from the office to which such jurisdiction is attached; by administrative removal from the office; by punitive deprivation of the office; by transfer to another office; by the lapse of time predetermined for the holding of office; or by the death of the officeholder.[4]

Let it be supposed, however, that the superior who inflicted this penalty *ad beneplacitum* was not subsequently shorn of his power in any of the divers ways enumerated above. In that event the penalty could still cease in another way, namely, by dispensation. Cessation of the penalty by dispensation might also occur when a temporary deprivation of the garb had been inflicted for a definite number of months or years and the superior later saw fit to dispense from its observance before the *terminus ad quem* had been reached.[5] With this last mentioned mode of cessation, however, a difficulty arises. The law of the Code states that vindicative penalties cease by dispensation granted by him who possesses the power of so dispensing according to the norm of canon 2236.[6]

There exist two schools of thought, however, relative to the question of just who is the proper dispensatory power designated by canon 2236, when the vindicative penalty to be dispensed from is one which has been established in the common law of the Code as a *ferendae sententiae* penalty. Since temporary deprivation of the clerical garb, of its very nature, is such a penalty, the controversy concerning the remission of the whole general class must perforce extend itself to any treatment of a possible dispensation from this one particular species of that class. Perpetual deprivation of the garb likewise is but another species of the same general class; accordingly, any discussion concerning dispensation from it too must of necessity partake in the general controversy. Wherefore, it has been deemed best by the writer to defer the treatment of the cessation of temporary deprivation of the garb by means of dispensation to a later article, where it will be expounded *ex professo* in conjunction with dispensation from perpetual deprivation.

---

[4] Canons 183-195.

[5] Canon 2289: "Poena vindicativa finitur . . . eius dispensatione ab eo concessa qui legitimam habeat dispensandi potestatem ad normam can. 2236."

[6] Canon 2289.

Lastly, by way of transition to the writer's discussion on the cessation of perpetual deprivation of the garb, it need hardly be mentioned that temporary deprivation ceases with the death of the delinquent, if that event should occur before the penalty's cessation in any of the other ways already mentioned.

ARTICLE 2. CESSATION OF PERPETUAL DEPRIVATION OF THE CLERICAL GARB

From the very terminology used in the penal legislation of the Code relative to the vindicative penalty of perpetual deprivation of the clerical garb, one would reasonably presume that this penalty, once inflicted, is never subject to cessation or remission during the delinquent's lifetime.[7] Such a presumption, moreover, would be entirely in accord with the primary norm for the doctrinal interpretation of ecclesiastical laws as stated in the first book of the Code, viz., ecclesiastical laws are to be understood according to the proper signification of the words employed, considered in their text and context.[8]

Added assurance of the validity of such a presumption would also derive from the fact that the infliction of deposition, as has already been pointed out, is always required as a prerequisite before the legitimate ecclesiastical superior can proceed to punish further a delinquent and contumacious cleric with the added penalty of perpetual deprivation of his distinctive garb.[9] Consequently, one could feel that if the penalty of perpetual deprivation of the clerical garb were ever to be dispensed from, such a dispensation would be granted only in conjunction with a dispensation from the penalty of the deposition which had been inflicted prior to it. For the remission of the deposition, however, the deposed cleric would have to manifest a radical change in his attitude. What reasonable hope could one have of such a radical change when the cleric involved has already had his penalty of deposition augmented with

[7] Canon 2298, 11°: "Poenae vindicativae quae clericis tantum applicantur, sunt: . . . privatio *perpetua* habitus ecclesiastici" and canon 2304, § 1: ". . . Ordinarius potest eum *perpetuo* privare iure deferendi habitum ecclesiasticum."

[8] Canon 18.

[9] Canon 2304, § 1: "Si clericus *depositus*. . . ."

perpetual deprivation of his clerical garb, and that precisely because of obdurate incorrigibility? Furthermore, deposition, like perpetual deprivation of the garb, is of its very nature perpetual in character.[10]

Regardless of the validity of any such presumption, however, and granted also the fact that a cleric of such caliber shows little likelihood of ever repenting and performing penance, one must never fail to take into consideration the inscrutable wonders wrought in the hearts of even the most hardened sinners through the influence of divine grace. Perhaps under the influence of actual grace, the deposed and defrocked cleric will one day come to rue the crime which he has committed and his obstinate refusal to amend. What then could be done to restore him to his former state? Could these two *perpetual* penalties, in other words, ever be the subject of a subsequent dispensation?

To answer these two questions, one must consider the purpose of vindicative penalties in general, of which class these two penalties are specific types. While it is true that vindicative penalties have as their primary object the expiation of a delict and the restoration of the public order,[11] so much so that their remission does not depend on the cessation of the delinquent's contumacy,[12] as is the case with censures,[13] still they do not necessarily exclude from their purpose the correction and emendation of the delinquent upon whom they have been inflicted. The truth of this statement is evidenced by the fact that the Code permits the judge to refrain from executing the sentence in the case of certain vindicative penalties, when the mitigating circumstances delineated by the Code are verified in the case under consideration.[14] Conversely, the Church's medicinal penalties or censures—excommunication, suspension, and interdict (the latter two

[10] Cf. Berutti, *De Delictis et Poenis,* p. 234, n. 90V; Findlay, *Deposition and Degradation,* pp. 133, 134, 200.

[11] Canon 2286: "Poenae vindicativae illae sunt, quae directe ad delicti expiationem tendunt. . . ."

[12] Canon 2286: ". . . ita ut earum remissio e cessatione contumaciae delinquentis non pendeat."

[13] Canon 2248, § 2.

[14] Canon 2288.

when used as censures)—are primarily concerned with the amendment of the delinquent rather than with the expiation of the delict and the restoration of public order.[15] Consequently, absolution from the censure must be granted by the competent ecclesiastical authority once the censure has achieved its purpose, i.e., once it has become apparent that the delinquent has receded from his contumacy and is now desirous of absolution.[16]

These penalties, however, do not exclude from their ambit, albeit secondarily and indirectly, the expiation of the delict and the restoration of the public order. Attesting to the verity of this latter statement is the fact that the Code allows the superior who absolves from a censure to impose a fitting vindicative penalty or penance in place of the censure, if the circumstances of the case warrant such an action.[17] With all reputable canonists, one may conclude that there exists a twofold purpose in all ecclesiastical penalties. In imposing medicinal penalties the Church's main purpose is the correction and emendation of the delinquent; in inflicting vindicative penalties, its primary concern is the expiation of the delict and the restoration of the public order. But neither type of penalty entirely excludes as a proper secondary end the principal purpose of the other type of penalty.[18] The Code itself, in defining ecclesiastical penalties in general, bears out this opinion.[19]

Accordingly, if it should happen that a cleric, deposed and perpetually deprived of his clerical garb, would sincerely repent and perform fitting penance, there would be a possibility of his

---

[15] Canon 2241, § 1.

[16] Canon 2248, § 2: "Absolutio denegari nequit cum primum delinquens a contumacia recesserit ad normam can. 2242, § 3; . . ."

[17] Canon 2248, § 2: ". . . a censura autem absolvens, potest, si res ferat, pro patrato delicto congruam vindicativam poenam vel poenitentiam infligere."

[18] Cf. Roberti, *De Poenis in Genere,* n. 223, pp. 247-250; n. 231, p. 264; n. 232, p. 265; Woywod, *Commentary,* II, 424-425; 454; Sole, *Praelectiones in Lib. V, Codicis Iuris Canonici, De Delictis et Poenis* (Romae: Pustet, 1920), pp. 187-188, n. 263 (hereafter cited as *De Delictis et Poenis*).

[19] Canon 2215: "Poena ecclesiastica est privatio alicuius boni ad delinquentis correctionem *et* delicti punitionem a legitima auctoritate inflicta." Note the Code's choice of the coordinating conjunction *et* in preference to the disjunctive *vel* in its Latin text.

being granted a dispensation from both penalties. One may ask how this would come about. Certainly, it would not be through absolution by a competent ecclesiastical superior, since both deposition and perpetual deprivation of the clerical garb are vindicative penalties, and not dependent for their remission on the delinquent's recession from contumacy, as stated above.[20] Neither could the delinquent cleric's confessor suspend the obligation of observing the penalty in question in a more urgent occult case, viz., when observance of the penalty would expose the deposed and defrocked cleric to infamy and scandal. Such a power is indeed granted to confessors by the Code, but only in regard to *latae sententiae* vindicative penalties when the case is occult.[21]

As has already been pointed out, perpetual deprivation of the clerical garb is never inflicted as a *latae sententiae* penalty or in occult cases. Since these two conditions are not verified in the penalty under discussion, the confessor enjoys no power whatsoever with regard to its observance by the cleric so punished. Even *in articulo mortis* the confessor enjoys no special prerogatives as to the remission of this penalty. The Code does indeed grant special faculties to all confessors at this sacred time, but only with reference to the absolution of sins and censures howsoever they may have been reserved.[22] Nothing is said concerning the remission of *vindicative* penalties. Remission of perpetual deprivation of the clerical garb, moreover, would be entirely unnecessary when the delinquent cleric is at the point of death, since by its legal nature this penalty ceases with the death of the cleric so punished, and in no wise hinders the reconciliation of the soul with God.

In establishing perpetual deprivation of the clerical garb as one of its vindicative penalties peculiar to clerics, the Church, in the person of the Supreme Pontiff under whose authority the Code of Canon Law was promulgated, has already determined beforehand the length of time necessary in expiation of the grave crimes and consequent incorrigibility which warranted the infliction of so serious a penalty. Ordinarily the period of expiation will consist of the remainder of the offender's life here on earth. Perpetual

[20] Canons 2236, § 1, and 2286.

[21] Canon 2290.

[22] Canon 882.

deprivation of the delinquent cleric's garb is inflicted not to be subsequently dispensed from; rather, it is to be borne until death, so that from the enduring of it the perturbation of the public order which the scandalous conduct of the defrocked cleric caused may as far as possible be repaired. Nonetheless, if later on in the delinquent cleric's life he should manifest sincere repentance and amendment by his changed mode of life, perpetual deprivation of his clerical garb, like all other vindicative penalties, can be remitted by the competent ecclesiastical authority.[23]

With regard to the penalty in question, the determination of the competent ecclesiastical superior according to the norm of canon 2236 for the granting of a dispensation is a matter of dispute, as has already been pointed out in the preceding article on the cessation of temporary deprivation by way of dispensation. This controversy will be discussed somewhat at length in the following article.

ARTICLE 3. CESSATION OF THE PENALTY BY DISPENSATION

It is with the cessation of this penalty by means of a dispensation that a difficulty is encountered. As has already been pointed out in an earlier chapter of this dissertation, both temporary and perpetual deprivation of the garb are *ferendae sententiae* penalties in their nature. Now, *ferendae sententia* vindicative penalties are of two types: those which derive *a iure* and those which derive *ab homine. A iure* derived penalties are those which are determined and established by law, whether that law be universal or particular, or merely by an ordinance *ad modum legis,* i.e., in the form of a general precept.[24] *Ab homine* derived penalties, on the other hand, are those which, though they be established by law, are inflicted by means of a particular precept given by the

[23] Canon 2289: "Poena vindicativa finitur eius expiatione vel dispensatione ab eo concessa qui legitimam habeat dispensandi potestatem ad normam can. 2236." Cf. also canon 123 (in reference to the loss of the clerical privileges): "Memoratis privilegiis clericus . . . amittit, si . . . privatione perpetua iuris deferendi habitum ecclesiasticum plectatur, ad normam can. . . . 2304; recuperat vero, si haec poena remittatur. . . ."

[24] Canon 2217, § 1, 3°; cf. Berutti, *De Delictis et Poenis,* p. 66; Wernz-Vidal, *Ius Canonicum,* VII, n. 146, nota 16.

competent superior or by means of a condemnatory judicial sentence.[25] In consequence of this distinction, therefore, both species of deprivation of the clerical garb may be considered as *a iure* derived penalties, in so far as they are established by the common law of the Code in punishment of a specific delict.[26]

The specific delict for which by specification of the Code they are to serve as punishment is incorrigible obduracy in scandalous conduct. This specific object is qualified in both temporary and perpetual deprivation. In temporary deprivation of the garb, it consists of incorrigible scandalous conduct in general, which can be removed in no other way than by the infliction of this penalty. In perpetual deprivation of the garb, it consists in scandalous incorrigibility after deposition for one or the other of the specific crimes punished by the law of the Code with deposition. When such scandalous incorrigibility on the part of a delinquent cleric does present itself in a practical case, both species of the penalty in question qualify as deriving *a iure tantum* as long as nothing is done to combat the situation. The proper remedies to be applied when such practical cases do arise, as was pointed out in the preceding chapter on procedure, are the imposition of a particular precept when the case in question is notorious in fact, and the passing of a condemnatory judicial sentence when the case in question is merely public. Once such action has been taken, however, both species of the penalty cease to derive *a iure tantum,* and become penalties deriving *a iure et ab homine,* but they are thenceforth considered as deriving *ab homine.*[27] In all practical cases, therefore, the penalty will be treated as a penalty deriving *ab homine.*

It is precisely because of this fact that the difficulty arises relative to a subsequent dispensation from either species of the penalty, if and when changed circumstances should warrant such a move. The difficulty consists in this. The law of the Code enacts one general norm for the remission of all penalties alike in canon 2236, whether those penaltes be vindicative or medicinal,

[25] Canon 2217, § 1, 3°.
[26] Canons 2300 and 2304.
[27] Canon 2217, § 1, 3°.

ferendae or *latae sententiae* in nature.[28] But in addition to this one general norm for the cessation of penalties, the Code also enacts specific norms for the remission of *latae sententiae* censures,[29] *ferendae sententiae censures,*[30] and *latae sententiae* vindicative penalties.[31]

As to dispensations from *ferendae sententiae* vindicative penalties, however, no special norm other than the norm laid down in canon 2236 for the dispensation from all vindicative penalties in general is given. Accordingly, in virtue of canon 2289, dispensation from both species of this *ferendae sententiae* vindicative penalty of deprivation of the clerical garb, like dispensation from all other penalties of the same class, is reserved to him who has the legitimate power of so dispensing, as indicated in canon 2236. But in reference to the class of penalties in question, one may well ask: just who is the competent superior, possessed of the power granted by canon 2236, to whom such dispensations are reserved? In other words, is the dispensation from deprivation of the clerical garb reserved to the one (namely, the Roman Pontiff) who established it in the common law of the Code as the penalty to be applied in the circumstances therein described, or is it reserved to the delinquent's proper ordinary (e.g., the local ordinary, the major superior of exempt clerical religious, etc.), who actually inflicted the penalty by decreeing the particular precept (in the supposition of a factually notorious case) or by whose authority the judge or collegiate tribunal of judges passed the condemnatory sentence (in the supposition of an ordinary public case)? Or, are these two species of this *ferendae sententiae penalty,* once they have been properly inflicted and thus derive *ab homine,* to be treated in the same way as *ab homine* deriving censures? Is their dispensation in the nature of *ab homine* derived penalties reserved to the one who inflicted them by way of particular precept or

---

[28] Canon 2236, § 1: "Remissio poenae sive per absolutionem, si agatur de censuris, sive per dispensationem, si de poenis vindicativis, concedi tantum potest ab eo qui poenam tulit, vel ab eius competente Superiore aut successore, vel ab eo cui haec potestas commissa est."

[29] Canon 2245, § 4.

[30] Canon 2245, § 2.

[31] Canon 2237.

condemnatory sentence, in much the same way as *ab homine* inflicted censures are reserved?[32]

There are two schools of thought on the solution to this problem. The whole question reduces itself to the interpretation which one makes of the clause *"qui poenam tulit"* in canon 2236, § 1. The key word *tulit* is translated by the members of the first school of thought as "establish." If the term be thus understood, then canon 2236, § 1, would of necessity restrict the power of dispensation from deprivation of the garb to him who had established this penalty in the common law, namely the Roman Pontiff, his successor, or his delegate. The delinquent cleric's ordinary who inflicted the penalty by way of particular precept or condemnatory sentence (depending on the notoriety of the case in question) would have no power whatsoever as to the granting of a dispensation from its observance, even though that superior should enjoy full jurisdiction over the guilty party.

The proponents of this opinion give the following reasons for such an interpretation of the controverted text. First and foremost, the dispensation from any vindicative penalty (*a pari* from the specific penalty in question) is an act of favor, not of justice.[33] Consequently, the one punished with a vindicative penalty (e.g., the defrocked cleric) suffers no inconvenience in being compelled to seek the dispensation from his penalty from the one who established it in law, viz., the Pope in the case under consideration.[34]

Secondly, when an ordinary or a judge deputed by him (in the case of perpetual deprivation, the collegiate tribunal) inflicts a *ferendae sententiae* vindicative penalty established by the common law of the Church, he merely *applies* the penalty. Rather than say that the ordinary or his deputed judge *inflicts* deprivation of the garb then, the authors who interpret *tulit* as "establish" would hold that what he actually does is merely ascertain if the conditions required by the common law for the infliction of the penalty are actually verified in the case at hand and, if he finds that they

[32] Canon 2245, § 2: "Censura ab homine est reservata ei qui censuram inflixit aut sententiam tulit, eiusve Superiori competenti, vel successori aut delegato. . . ."

[33] Cf., e.g., Lega, *De Delictis et Poenis,* nn. 121-123.

[34] Cf. Lega, *op. cit.,* n. 129.

are indeed verified, then he merely applies the penalty already set down by the law as the punishment to be meted out for such a delict.[35]

If this were true, then the conclusion drawn by these canonists would certainly be justified, for in reality the ordinary would be acting only as a judge, and canon 2236, § 3, explicitly states that a judge who *ex officio* applies a penalty constituted by his superior is incapable of remitting the penalty once it has been applied.[36] This opinion was certainly held by Lega[37] (1860-1935) and later by Findlay.[38] Other reputable canonists apparently incline towards the same opinion, but their failure to fortify their belief with tangible arguments and their loose use of terminology leave room for doubt.[39]

If, on the other hand, one translates the term *tulit* in the sense of "inflict" or "establish and inflict," then canon 2236, § 1, would admit of a dispensation from the penalty in question by the superior who inflicted it by way of particular precept, or by whose authority the judge or collegiate tribunal of judges passed the condemnatory sentence (again depending on the notoriety of the case and which species of the penalty was in question), even though the penalty had been established by the common law of the Church. This seems to be the opinion of the vast majority of commentators, though clarity of expression and consistency in following out the principle established by this opinion to its logical conclusions are woefully wanting.[40]

---

[35] Cf. Lega, *loc. cit.*

[36] Canon 2236, § 3.

[37] Cf. *De Delictis et Poenis,* nn. 129, 130.

[38] Cf. *Deposition and Degradation,* pp. 200, 201.

[39] Cf., e.g., De Meester, *Compendium,* III, nn. 1726-1799 and Cance, *Le Code de Droit Canonique* (2. ed., 3 vols., Paris: Libraire Lecoffre, Gabalda, 1929), III, n. 212.

[40] Cf., e.g., Augustine, *Commentary,* VIII, pp. 239, 240; Ayrinhac, *Penal Legislation,* nn. 65, 70; Woywod, *Commentary,* II, nn. 2076, 2077; Wernz-Vidal, *Ius Canonicum,* VII, nn. 211, 329, 258, 367; Berutti, *De Delictis et Poenis,* n. 38, II; Coronata, *Institutiones,* IV, nn. 1736, 1737; Blat, *Commentarium,* V, nn. 58, 59; Vermeersch-Creusen, *Epitome,* III, nn. 430, 491; Chelodi, *Ius Poenale,* nn. 29, 47; Sipos, *Enchiridion,* § 232, n. 2; Salucci, *Il Diritto Penale,* I, p. 164, n. 3; p. 300, n. 2; Sole, *De Delictis et Poenis,* n. 147.

The following reasons are adduced in favor of this latter translation of *tulit*. First, in other places in the Code the universal legislator actually employs the verb *ferre* in the sense of "inflict"[41] and in the sense of "establish and inflict."[42] Moreover, if one were to translate the word *tulit* as used in canon 2236, § 1, in the exclusive sense of "establish," an absurdity in the law itself would arise. This is evident from the fact that the canon in question has been set down by the universal lawgiver as the general norm for the remission of *all* ecclesiastical penalties, censures and vindicative penalties alike.

If one interpreted the word *tulit* exclusively as "establish," however, this general norm for the remission of censures could in no way be applied to censures because of the conflict which would then arise between it and the more specific norms found in the Code for the absolution from censures. It would not apply to *latae sententiae* censures, since such censures are never reserved to the one who enacted the law or gave the precept to which they are attached, unless such reservation is expressly stated in the law or precept.[43] Neither would it be applicable to *ferendae sententiae* censures, for (again by express provision of the common law) such censures are reserved not to the one who enacted the law or gave the precept to which they are attached, but rather to the superior who inflicted them or passed the condemnatory sentence.[44] Such an absurdity in the law is unthinkable. Consequently, one must strive to reconcile the seeming contradiction by resorting to the *Normae Generales* of the First Book of the Code.

In the primary norm for the doctrinal interpretation of the laws of the Code one finds that ecclesiastical laws are to be understood

41 Cf., e.g., canon 2242, § 1: ". . . potest . . . ferri censura etiam in delinquentes ignotos."

42 Cf., e.g., canon 2247, § 1: "Si censura Sedi Apostolicae reservata sit, Ordinarius nequit aliam censuram sibi reservatam in idem delictum ferre."

43 Canon 2245, § 4: "Censura latae sententiae non est reservata, nisi in lege vel praecepto id expresse dicatur; et in dubio sive iuris sive facti reservatio non urget."

44 Canon 2245, § 2: "Censura ab homine est reservata ei qui censuram inflixit aut sententiam tulit, eiusve Superiori competenti, vel successori, aut delegato. . . ."

according to the proper signification of the words employed, considered in both their text and context. If the law still remains doubtful, then one must look to parallel passages in the Code, if there be any.[45] For the remission of *ab homine* derived vindicative penalties, the logical parallel passage seems to be the law relating to the absolution from *ab homine* inflicted censures. Granted that there are many differences between absolution from a censure and dispensation from a vindicative penalty, still there is a great deal of similarity. If one adapted the principle delineated in canon 2245, § 2, for the remission of *ab homine* inflicted censures to the remission of *ab homine* derived vindicative penalties in canon 2236, and translated the word *tulit* of the latter canon as "establish or inflict," or simply as "inflict" (as it certainly should be translated in canon 2245, § 2), the absurdity would disappear.

Granted even that this would constitute an illicit use of canon 18, one could still adduce the probative value of canon 15, which states that in a doubt of law ecclesiastical laws are not binding. There is enough weight of authority on both sides of the question to constitute a truly probable doubt of law. Accordingly, one could safely hold that the dispensation from *ab homine* derived vindicative penalties as established by the common law can be granted not only by the Sovereign Pontiff who established them, but also by the intermediate ordinary who inflicted them. This argument is enhanced by the interpretation which many canonists give to canon 15.

Noted commentators on the law of the Code, such as Michiels,[46] adapt rule 57 of the Rules of Law given by Pope Boniface VIII at the end of his *Liber Sextus* to their interpretation of this canon. This rule, which in its application refers directly to the conditions and obligations of contracts[47] rather than to laws in general, reads as follows: *"contra eum, qui legem dicere potuit apertius, est interpretatio facienda."* It presupposes that the terms stating the conditions and obligations of a contract should be in clear language, which will not allow of misinterpretation. If such is not the case, then one can apply this rule, so that the party to the

[45] Canon 18.

[46] *Normae Generales,* I, 335.

[47] Cf. Reiffenstuel, *Ius Canonicum Universum,* V, Reg. LVII, n. 2.

contract who could have clarified the terms, but did not, must suffer whatever detriment is involved in a less advantageous interpretation of these terms by the other party. By adaptation of this rule to the enactment of laws, responsibility for clarity of terminology is transferred to the lawgiver in virtue of his office. As a result, if he should use ambiguous terminology in enacting a law (as is the case with the infelicitous choice of *tulit* in canon 2236, § 1), then he must allow the less rigorous interpretation of these terms. In other words, in the case at hand, by an adaptation of rule 57 in the interpretation of canon 15, the Sovereign Pontiff can not (i.e., in virtue of canon 2236, § 1, as stated now) urge the reservation of the *ab homine* derived penalty of deprivation of the clerical garb exclusively to himself to the detriment of the intermediate ordinary who inflicted the penalty.[48]

Negatively, one may add that the chief argument offered by the proponents of the first opinion, viz., that the ordinary in inflicting this type of penalty is acting merely as a judge who applies the penalty, is fallacious. In reality, he acts not merely as a judge, but as a jurisdictional superior with full jurisdiction over the delinquent cleric.[49] In the ordinary case, it is true, the judge or collegiate tribunal chosen by the ordinary to hear the case and to pass sentence does merely apply the penalty. But the judge in question and the members of that tribunal possess no power of jurisdiction over the defrocked cleric in the external forum other than that of exercising their office of judging.[50] Such, however, is not the case with the superior who constitutes the judge or the members of the collegiate tribunal. He, like the ordinary who inflicts deprivation of the garb by way of particular precept in a notorious case, must have complete jurisdiction over the delinquent cleric.[51] The *vinculum poenale* of the *ferendae sententiae* penalty in question is not established until he actually inflicts the penalty by way of particular precept or condemnatory sentence. In any practical case of dispensation from the penalty, therefore,

[48] Cf. Roelker, "An Introduction to the Rules of Law," Part I, *The Jurist,* X (n. 3, July, 1950), 294-296.

[49] Cf. Berutti, *De Delictis et Poenis,* n. 38, VI.

[50] Cf. Berutti, *loc. cit.*

[51] Canons 2217, § 1, 2°; 2220, § 1.

it is of him that one could say, *tulit poenam,* and consequently he has the power of dispensing from its further observance in virtue of the general norm laid down in canon 2236, § 1.[52]

In analyzing the arguments propounded by both sides, the writer of the present dissertation feels constrained to concur with the view expressed by the protagonists of the latter opinion. More specifically, he holds that the delinquent cleric's proper ordinary, though he be subordinate to the one who established the penalty of deprivation of the clerical garb in the common law of the Code, is nonetheless empowered to dispense such a cleric from further observance of the penalty which he (the ordinary) had inflicted by way of extrajudicial precept or condemnatory sentence.

Before this article be brought to a close, a few words are in order on a matter of practical importance in the case of an ordinary who has seen fit to inflict perpetual deprivation of the ecclesiastical garb. While it seems to the writer that such an ordinary would be perfectly within his rights in remitting this penalty by way of dispensation, when and if the delinquent cleric upon whom he had inflicted it had perfectly repaired the scandal given, and had amended his way of life, still one wonders about the prudence of such a course of action. In the preceding article, it was hinted that a dispensation from a perpetual deprivation of the garb should be granted only in conjunction with a dispensation from the penalty of deposition, which of necessity must have been inflicted prior to it.

Now Findlay, in his discussion of a possible dispensation from the penalty of deposition, maintains that such a dispensation is reserved to the Sovereign Pontiff alone or to his specially deputed delegate.[53] He bases this conclusion on the translation of *tulit* in canon 2236, § 1, as "establish." The present writer agrees with him in the conclusion reached, viz., that a dispensation from deposition is reserved to the Pope, but does not admit the premise on which Findlay has drawn his conclusion. Rather, for the foundation of the reservation to the Pope of this *ferendae sententiae* vindicative penalty of deposition he looks to the argument drawn

---

[52] Cf., e.g., Wernz-Vidal, *Ius Canonicum,* VII, nn. 209, 211; Berutti, *De Delictis et Poenis,* n. 38; Salucci, *Il Diritto Penale,* I, p. 164, n. 3.

[53] Cf. *Deposition and Degradation,* p. 201.

by practically all authors from the reservation to the Sovereign Pontiff in public cases of any *latae sententiae* vindicative penalty containing a disqualification for office.[54] Deposition, as Findlay is careful to point out, is inflicted only in public cases and contains just such an automatic disqualification for office.[55]

Another argument can be drawn (at least with reference to four of the ten cases in which deposition can be inflicted) from the fact that infamy of law may also be present, and that the dispensation from this penalty is reserved to the Apostolic See.[56] Infamy of law is incurred as a *latae sententiae* penalty for desecration of the Sacred Species and for the violation of graves. In both of these cases deposition is also prescribed with preceptive words as a *ferendae sententiae* penalty if the culprit be a cleric.[57]

Infamy of law must be declared in the case of apostasy, heresy, or schism after admonition, and in the case of certain crimes against the sixth commandement. In the former case deposition is prescribed with preceptive words, and in the latter case with

---

[54] Cf., e.g., Cloran, *Previews and Practical Cases,* p. 205: "When penalties involving incapacity for . . . offices . . . (canon 2237, § 1, 3°) automatically result by law, as for example, from the vindicative penalty of deposition (canon 2303, § 1) . . . inflicted by a diocesan court of five judges (canon 1576, § 1, 2°), the dispensation from the vindicative penalty is reserved to the Holy See (cf. canon 2286). Whether, in the case of other *ferendae sententiae* vindicative penalties of the Code, Ordinaries can dispense from such penalties once they have been inflicted by a diocesan court is disputed. The affirmative opinion as given by Sole and others seems correct and preferable in practice." Cf. also Ayrinhac, *Penal Legislation,* p. 132, n. 175; Coronata, *Institutiones,* IV, p. 276, n. 1836; canon 2237, § 1, 3°: "In casibus publicis potest Ordinarius poenas latae sententiae iure communi statutas remittere, exceptis: . . . 3°. Poenis inhabilitatis ad beneficia, officia, . . ."

[55] Cf. *Deposition and Degradation,* pp. 129-131, 190.

[56] Canon 2295: "Infamia iuris desinit sola dispensatione a Sede Apostolica concessa; . . ."

[57] Canons 2320: "Qui species consecratas abiecerit vel ad malum finem abduxerit aut retinuerit, est suspectus de haeresi; incurrit in excommunicationem latae sententiae specialissimo modo Sedi Apostolicae reservatam; est ipso facto infamis, et clericus praeterea est deponendus," and 2328: "Qui cadavera vel sepulcra mortuorum ad furtum vel alium malum finem violaverit, interdicto personali puniatur, sit ipso facto infamis, et clericus praeterea deponatur."

facultative words, if the delinquent be a cleric.[58] Accordingly, if deposition had been inflicted for any one of these four delicts, the dispensation therefrom would be reserved to the Sovereign Pontiff not only because of the incapacity for office involved in deposition itself, but also because of the same incapacity involved in infamy of law, which had been incurred *ipso facto* or had been declared by judicial sentence.[59]

It may be objected that this same incapacity for office, from which by special reservation the Supreme Pontiff alone can dispense when the case is public, as well as infamy of law in the four cases mentioned, is present not only in the case of a deposed cleric, but also in the case of a deposed cleric who has been further punished with perpetual deprivation of his clerical garb. If deposition be reserved, then, with reference to the granting of a dispensation from it, why should not the same be true with reference to perpetual deprivation of the garb?

A distinction must be made. With regard to six of the delicts punished by deposition, incapacity for office is a direct result of the infliction of this penalty. With regard to the other four delicts punished by deposition, incapacity for office either had already been incurred automatically on commission of the delict before the penalty of deposition was inflicted by way of condemnatory sentence, or has been declared to exist at the same time that the deposition was inflicted by way of condemnatory sentence. In either of these last two suppositions, however, it was the same delict which occasioned both penalties. The same does not hold true with reference to the perpetual deprivation of the clerical garb. When this penalty is inflicted, the penalties reserved to the

---

[58] Canons 2314, § 1, 2°: "Omnes a christiana fide apostatae et omnes et singuli haeretici aut schismatici: . . . 2°. Nisi moniti resipuerint, priventur beneficio, dignitate, pensione, officio aliove munere, si quod in Ecclesia habeant, infames declarentur, et clerici, iterata monitione, deponantur; . . ." and 2359, § 2: "Si delictum admiserint (clerici in sacris) contra sextum decalogi praeceptum cum minoribus infra aetatem sexdecim annorum, vel adulterium, stuprum, bestialitatem, sodomiam, lenocinium, incestum cum consangiuneis aut affinibus in primo gradu exercuerint, suspendantur, infames declarentur, quolibet officio, beneficio, dignitate, munere, si quod habeant, priventur, et in casibus gravioribus deponantur."

[59] Canon 2294, § 1: "Qui infamia iuris laborat, . . . est inhabilis ad obtinenda beneficia, pensiones, officia et dignitates ecclesiasticas, . . ."

Holy See for dispensation (incapacity for office and infamy of law) are already present. Perpetual deprivation of the garb has nothing to do with bringing them into existence.

In view of the preceding remarks, is it advisable for an ordinary to dispense from the one penalty which he has the power of dispensing from, when he can not dispense from the other which in the case is necessarily concomitant? It appears to the writer that such a course of action would be somewhat imprudent. Rather, the ordinary should refer the whole matter to the Holy See, much as the Code commands it to be done in the case of dispensations from matrimonial impediments when the ordinary has dispensatory power over some only of the impediments present in a particular case.[60]

It could be objected that this is an application of the rule: When an express prescript of law is wanting concerning a certain matter, the norm is to be taken from laws enacted in similar cases, and that the application of this rule is invalid in penal matters.[61] Such an objection cannot be sustained, since the restriction placed on the use of this rule is in relation to the application of penalties, and not in relation to their remission.[62]

Neither could one object that the cleric is being deprived unnecessarily of his right to wear the cleric's distinctive garb between the time he applies for a dispensation from his penalty and the *terminus ad quem* of the time it takes to receive a favorable reply from Rome. It must be remembered that all dispensations from vindicative penalties are a matter of favor, and that the defrocked cleric has no intrinsic right to receive such a favor. Moreover, by meriting the infliction of such a dread penalty, he has forfeited the right which every cleric has of wearing a distinctive garb. The mere fact that he has now reformed and has promised to do better does not alter his juridical status. He still remains without any right to the restoration of his clerical garb. On the part of the ordinary who inflicted the penalty, therefore, prudence seems to dictate the non-use of his dispensatory power with reference to the vindicative penalty whereby a cleric has sustained the perpetual deprivation of his ecclesiastical garb.

[60] Canon 1050.

[61] Canon 20.

[62] Canon 20: ". . . nisi agatur de poenis *applicandis*. . . ."

CONCLUSIONS

Since deprivation of the clerical garb as a *specific* vindicative penalty peculiar to clerics has been in existence only from the time of the enactment of the Code of Canon Law, the following conclusions may be of help.

A. General Historical Conclusions

1. Prior to the enactment of the Code of Canon Law, deposition and degradation were the penalties which served for the punishing of scandalous and incorrigible conduct on the part of delinquent clerics, which crimes are now punished through deprivation of the clerical garb (pp. 14-18; 28-33; 42-43; 46-50).
2. Similarly, deposition and degradation were the penalties which, prior to 1918, entailed the chief effect that now is ascribed to deprivation of the clerical garb, namely the loss of the clerical privileges (pp. 18-26; 33-36; 37-42; 44-46; 50-52).

B. Specific Historical Conclusions

1. The Generic Character of Deprivation of the Clerical Garb Prior to the Code of Canon Law
   a. Before the end of the fifth or the beginning of the sixth century, deprivation of the clerical garb could not have existed even as an *implicit* part of the more generic penalties of deposition and degradation (pp. 4-6; 9-10).
   b. After the beginning of the sixth century up to the time of Pope Boniface VIII (1294-1303), deprivation of the clerical garb should probably be considered as implicit in these penalties, whenever the prevention of further scandal by the sequestration of the deposed cleric in a monastery was found to be impractical or impossible (pp. 10-13; 28-33).
   c. After the time of Boniface and his distinction between verbal

and actual degradation, deprivation of the clerical garb was an explicit part of the ceremony observed in the infliction of actual degradation (pp. 43-44).

2. The Effect of Deposition and Degradation on the Clerical Privileges.
   a. Up to the twelfth century, deposition and degradation alike resulted in the loss of the *privilegium immunitatis* alone (pp. 18-26; 33-36).
   b. While deposition and degradation in the first twelve centuries did not effect the loss of the privileged forum, civil legislation often provided that a cleric deposed by an ecclesiastical tribunal was to be punished by the secular courts (pp. 19-22).
   c. With the distinction made by Pope Innocent III at the end of the twelfth century between deposition and degradation, only the latter resulted in the loss of the clerical privileges (pp. 38-42).
   d. From this time onward all four clerical privileges were lost as a result of degradation.
   e. After the distinction by Pope Boniface VIII in the fourteenth century between verbal and actual degradation, only the latter effected the loss of the clerical privileges (pp. 43-44).
   f. From the time of the same distinction between verbal and actual degradation up to the enactment of the Code of Canon Law, actual degradation was the *only* way in which a cleric could be deprived of his clerical privileges and his garb (pp. 43-44; 53).

C. Canonical Conclusions

1. In the United States, the clerical garb which is the object of this penalty is the black suit and the Roman collar worn on the street by all clerics, as well as the cassock and Roman collar worn indoors by secular clerics, and the religious habit worn indoors by clerics who are professed religious (pp. 7-9).
2. Except for the cases wherein danger of death is present, acts

of orders and acts of jurisdiction placed by a cleric temporarily deprived of his clerical garb are illicit; acts of orders placed by a perpetually defrocked cleric are illicit, while acts of jurisdiction placed by a cleric in the same condition are invalid (pp. 60-65).

3. Neither temporary nor perpetual deprivation of the clerical garb exempts the cleric so punished from his obligation of celibacy or also his duty of the daily recitation of the Divine Office (pp. 65-69).
4. Offices, benefices, etc., held by a cleric temporarily deprived of his garb are not lost through such a deprivation; they have already been lost before a cleric is perpetually deprived of his right to wear his distinctive garb (pp. 69-70).
5. Temporary deprivation of the clerical garb has only an accidental bearing on the delinquent cleric's ecclesiastical revenue; perpetual deprivation effects a total loss of it (pp. 70-71).
6. Temporary deprivation of the garb effects only a penal suspension of the clerical privileges; perpetual deprivation, a true loss (pp. 71-74).
7. Neither temporary nor perpetual deprivation of the clerical garb impedes the reception of the sacraments of itself (pp. 74-76).
8. To inflict deprivation of the clerical garb, one must possess the power of jurisdiction in the external forum and ordinarily stand in the relationship of superior to subject with the cleric to be so punished (pp. 77-80).
9. The proper passive subject for the infliction of this penalty is a major cleric of the Latin rite, exclusive of the Roman Pontiff. The use of special procedural norms is mandatory in the cases involving bishops, cardinals, and apostolic legates (pp. 80-90).
10. Both the temporary and the perpetual deprivations of the clerical garb ordinarily require a judicial process for their infliction; temporary deprivation, before one judge; perpetual deprivation, before a collegiate tribunal of five judges (pp. 96-100; 118-122).
11. In cases of factual notoriety, the penalty can be inflicted with-

out any resorting to the usual criminal trial (pp. 100; 112-118).

12. The making of an appeal *in suspensivo* is granted to the defrocked cleric, except in the case wherein the penalty is inflicted in a factually notorious case (pp. 113; 122-123).
13. The superior who inflicts the penalty can dispense from its further observance; with regard to the perpetual deprivation of the garb, however, as a matter of prudence the superior should not so dispense (pp. 130-141).

BIBLIOGRAPHY

Sources

Acta Apostolicae Sedis, Commentarium Officiale, Romae, 1909-

Acta et Decreta Concilii Plenarii Baltimorensis III, A. D. MDCCCLXXXIV, Baltimorae: Typis Ioannis Murphy et Sociorum, 1886.

Bourcaren, T. Lincoln, *The Canon Law Digest,* 2 vols. and supplement through 1948, Milwaukee: Bruce, 1934, 1943, 1949.

Bruns, H. Th., *Canones Apostolorum et Conciliorum Saeculorum IV-VII,* 2 vols., Berlin: Reimeri, 1839.

Canones et Decreta Sacrosancti Oecumenici Concilii Tridentini, Romae: Ex Typographia Polyglotta S.C. de Propaganda Fide, 1882.

Codex Iuris Canonici Pii X Pontificis Maximi iussu digestus Benedicti Papae XV auctoritate promulgatus, Romae: Typis Polyglottis Vaticanis, 1917.

Codex Theodosianus cum perpetuis commentariis Iacobi Gothofredi, editio nova in VI tomos digesta, Lipsiae, 1743.

Codicis Iuris Canonici Fontes cura Emi Petri Card. Gasparri editi, 9 vols., Romae (postea Civitate Vaticana): Typis Polyglottis Vaticanis, 1923-1939. (Vols. VII-IX *ed. cura et studio Emi Iustiniani Card. Serédi.*)

Corpus Iuris Canonici, ed. Lipsiensis 2., Aemilius Ludovicus Richter—Aemilius Friedberg, ed. anastatice repetita, 2 vols., Lipsiae: Tauchnitz, 1928.

Corpus Iuris Civilis, 3 vols., Berolini: Apud Weidmannos, 1928-1929. Vol. I, *Institutiones,* ed. stereotypa 15. recognovit P. Krueger: *Digesta,* ed. stereotypa 15. recognovit Theodorus Mommsen; Vol. II, *Codex Iustinianus,* ed. stereotypa 10. recognovit et retractavit P. Krueger; Vol. III, *Novellae Constitutiones,* ed. stereotypa 5. R. Schoell; opus Schoellii morte interceptum absolvit G. Kroll.

Corpus Scriptorum Ecclesiasticorum Latinorum, Vindobonae: apud C. Geroldi Filium, Bibliopolam Academiae, 1866-

Decretum Gratiani emendatum et notationibus illustratum una cum glossis, Romae, 1582.

Hardouin, Jean, *Acta Conciliorum et Epistolae Decretales ac Constitutiones Summorum Pontificum,* 12 vols in 13, Parisiis, 1714-1715.

Jaffé, Philippus, *Regesta Pontificum Romanorum, ab condita ecclesia ad annum post Christum natum 1198,* 2. ed., correctam et auctam auspiciis Gulielmi Wattenbach curaverunt S. Loewenfeld, F. Kaltenbrunner, P. Ewald, 2 vols. in 1, Lipsiae, 1885-1888.

Mansi, Ioannes, *Sacrorum Conciliorum Nova et Amplissima Collectio,* 53 vols. in 59, Parisiis-Arnhem-Leipzig, 1901-1927.

Monumenta Germaniae Historica, Hannoverae-Lipsiae-Berolini, 1826-

———, *Epistolarum Sectio,* 7 toms. in 11 parts; Toms. I and II in 4 parts, *Gregorii I Papae, Registrum Epistolarum,* ediderunt P. Ewald et L. Hartmann, Berolini: apud Weidmannos, 1891-1899.

———, *Legum Sectio III, Concilia,* 2 toms. in 3 parts with suppl.; Tomus I, *Concilia Aevi Merovingici,* recensuit Fridericus Maassen, Hannoverae: impensis Bibliopolii Hahniani, 1893; Tomus II, pars prior, *Concilia Aevi Karolini,* recensuit Albertus Werminghoff, Hannoverae-Lipsiae: impensis Bibliopolii Hahniani, 1904.

———, *Legum Sectio IV, Constitutiones et Acta Publica Imperatorum et Regum,* 8 toms. in 17 parts; Tomus II, ed. L. Weiland, Hannoverae, 1896.

Sacrae Romanae Rotae Decisiones seu Sententiae (ab anno 1909), Romae: Typis Polyglottis Vaticanis, 1912-

Schroeder, H., *Canons and Decrees of the Council of Trent,* St. Louis: Herder, 1941.

Reference Works

Aichner, Simon, *Compendium Iuris Ecclesiastici,* 6. ed., Brixinae, 1887.

Ayrinhac, H. A., *Penal Legislation in the New Code of Canon Law,* revised by P. J. Lydon, New York: Benziger Brothers, 1936.

(Bachofen), Charles Augustine, *A Commentary on the New Code of Canon Law,* 8 vols., St. Louis: Herder, Vol. I, 6. ed., 1931; Vol. II, 6. ed., 1936; Vol. III, 5. ed., 1938; Vol. IV, 3. ed., 1925; Vol. V, 5. ed., 1938; Vol. VI, 3. ed., 1931; Vol. VII, 3. ed., 1930; Vol. VIII, 3. ed., 1931.

Barbosa, Augustinus, *Collectanea Doctorum tam Veterum quam Recentiorum in Ius Pontificium Universum,* 2 vols., Lugduni, 1716.

Baronius, Caesar, *Annales Ecclesiastici,* 37 vols., Barri-Ducis, 1864-1883.

Barrett, John D. M., *A Comparative Study of the Councils of Baltimore and the Code of Canon Law,* Catholic University of America Canon Law Studies, n. 83, Washington, D. C.: Catholic University of America, 1932.

Benedictus XIV, *De Synodo Dioecesana,* 2. ed., 2 vols., Parmae, 1764.

Berutti, Christophorus, *Institutiones Iuris Canonici,* 6 vols., Vol. VI, *De Delictis et Poenis,* Taurini-Romae: Marietti, 1938.

Beste, Udalricus, *Introductio in Codicem,* 3. ed., Collegeville, Minn.: St. John's Abbey Press, 1946.

Bingham, Joseph, *The Antiquities of the Christian Church,* 2 vols., London, 1856.

Blat, Albertus, *Commentarium Textus Codicis Iuris Cononici,* 5 vols. in 7, Romae: Collegio "Angelico"; Vol. I, 1921; Vol. II, pars I, ed. altera, 1921; Vol. II partes II et III, 3. ed., 1938; Vol. III, pars I, 2. ed., 1924; Vol. III, partes II-VI, 2. ed., 1934; Vol. IV, 1927; Vol. V, 1924.

Boak, Arthur, *A History of Rome to 565 A. D.*, 2. ed., New York: The Macmillan Co., 1938.

Bouix, Dominicus, *Tractatus de Episcopo, ubi et de Synodo Dioecesana*, 2. ed., Parisiis, 1873.

Cance, A., *Le Code de Droit Canonique*, 2. ed., 3 vols., Paris: Libraire Lecoffre, Gabalda, 1929.

Cappello, Felix M., *Tractatus Canonico-Moralis de Censuris iuxta Codicem Iuris Canonici*, 3. ed., Taurinorum Augustae: Marietti, 1933.

———, *Tractatus Canonico-Moralis de Sacramentis*, 5 vols., Taurinorum Augustae: Marietti, 1935-1945. Vol. I, *De Sacramentis in genere, de Baptismo, Confirmatione, et Eucharistia*, 5. ed., 1945; Vol. II, *De Poenitentia*, 5. ed., 1943.

Casey, James V., *A Study of Canon 2222, § 1*, Catholic University of America Canon Law Studies, n. 290, Washington, D. C.: Catholic University of America Press, 1949.

Catalanus, Iosephus, *Pontificale Romanum*, 3 vols., Parisiis, 1852.

Catholic Encyclopedia, The, 15 vols., index and 2 suppls., New York, 1907-1922.

Chelodi, Ioannes, *Ius Poenale et Ordo Procedendi in Iudiciis Criminalibus iuxta Codicem Iuris Canonici*, Tridenti, 1925 [1920?].

Christ, Joseph J., *Dispensation from Vindicative Penalties*, Catholic University of America Canon Law Studies, n. 174, Washington, D. C.: Catholic University of America Press, 1943.

Cloran, Owen M., *Previews and Practical Cases, Code of Canon Law, Book V, Delicts and Penalties*, Milwaukee: Bruce Publishing Co., 1951.

Cocchi, Guidus, *Commentarium in Codicem Iuris Canonici ad Usum Scholarum*, 8 vols., Taurinorum Augustae: Marietti, 1931-1940. Vol. I, 5. ed., 1938; Vol. II, 4. ed., 1937; Vol. III, 3. ed., 1931; Vol. IV, 3. ed., 1932; Vol. V, 3. ed., 1932; Vol. VI, 3. ed., 1933; Vol. VII, 3. ed., 1940; Vol. VIII, 4. ed., 1938.

Coronata, Matthaeus Conte a, *Institutiones Iuris Canonici*, 5 vols., Rome: Marietti: Vol. I, 3. ed., 1947; Vol. II, 3. ed., 1947; Vol. III, 3. ed., 1948; Vol. IV, 3. ed., 1947; Vol. V, 2. ed., 1947.

———, *Institutiones Iuris Canonici* (*Introductio*: *Ius Publicum Ecclesiasticum*), 3. ed., Rome: Marietti, 1948.

———, *Manuale Practicum Iuris Disciplinaris et Criminalis Regularium*, Taurini: Marietti, 1938.

De Meester, A., *Juris Canonici et Juris Canonico-Civilis Compendium*, nova ed., 3 vols. in 4, Brugis: Desclée, 1921-1928.

Devoti, Ioannes, *Institutionum Canonicarum Libri IV*, ed. prima Romana post quintam, Romae, 1825.

Dougherty, John W., *De Inquisitione Speciali*, Catholic University of America Canon Law Studies, n. 213, Washington, D. C.: Catholic University of America Press, 1945.

Downs, John E., *The Concept of Clerical Immunity,* Catholic University of America Canon Law Studies, n. 126, Washington, D. C.: Catholic University of America Press, 1941.

Du Cange, C., *Glossarium ad Scriptores Mediae et Infimae Latinitatis,* ed. nova, Parisiis, 1937-1938.

Durandus, Gulielmus, *Speculum Iuris cum Ioannis Andreae, Baldi de Ubaldis aliorumque aliquot praestantissimorum Iurisconsultorum Theorematibus,* Venetiis, 1577.

Eichmann, Eduard, *Das Strafrecht des Codex Iuris Canonici,* Paderborn: Ferdinand Schöningh, 1920.

Eidenschink, John, *The Election of Bishops in the Letters of Gregory the Great,* Catholic University of America Canon Law Studies, n. 215, Washington, D. C.: Catholic University of America Press, 1945.

Esswein, Anthony A., *The Extrajudicial Coercive Powers of Ecclesiastical Superiors,* Catholic University of America Canon Law Studies, n. 127, Washington, D. C.: Catholic University of America Press, 1941.

Fagnanus, Prosper, *Commentaria in Quinque Libros Decretalium,* 4 vols., Venetiis, 1697.

Faveville, *L'église et la royante en Angleterre,* Paris, 1944.

Ferraris, Lucius, *Prompta Bibliotheca, Canonica, Iuridica, Moralis, Theologica, necnon Ascetica, Polemica, Rubricistica, Historica,* 9 vols., Romae, 1885-1899.

Findlay, Stephen, *Canonical Norms Governing the Deposition and Degradation of Clerics,* Catholic University of America Canon Law Studies, n. 130, Washington, D. C.: Catholic University of America Press, 1941.

Grassis, Carolus de, *Tractatus de Effectibus Clericatus,* Venetiis, 1674.

Hefele, Charles J., *A History of the Christian Councils,* translated by Wm. Clark, 2. ed., 5 vols., Edinburgh, 1883-1896.

Hefele, Charles-LeClercq, Henri, *Histoire des Conciles,* 11 vols. in 20, Paris: Librairie Letouzey et Ané, 1907-1949.

Hilling, Nicholaus, *Das Personenrecht des Codex Iuris Canonici,* Paderborn: Ferdinand Schöningh, 1924.

Hinschius, Paul, *Das Kirchenrecht der Katholiken und Protestanten in Deutschland,* 6 vols., Berlin, 1869-1897. Vols. I-IV, *System des katholischen Kirchenrechts,* Berlin, 1869-1888.

———, *Decretales Pseudo-Isidorianae et Capitula Angilramni,* Lipsiae, 1863.

Hughes, P., *A History of the Church,* 2 vols., New York: Sheed and Ward, 1935.

Ioannes, Andreae, *In Quinque Decretalium Libros Novella Commentaria,* 4 vols., Venetiis, 1581.

Jolowicz, H., *Historical Introduction to the Study of Roman Law,* Cambridge: University Press, 1932.

Kelly, James P., *Jurisdiction of the Confessor According to the Code of Canon Law,* New York: Benziger Bros., 1929.

Kober, F. Q., *Die Deposition und Degradation nach den Grundsätzen des kirchlichen Rechts, historisch-dogmatisch dargestellt,* Tübingen, 1867.

Lega, Michael, *Praelectiones in Textum Iuris Canonici, De Iudiciis Ecclesiasticis,* 4 vols., Romae: Typis Vaticanis, 1896-1901.

———, *Praelectiones in Textum Iuris Canonici, De Delictis et Poenis,* 2. ed., Romae: ex Typographia Pontificia in Instituto Pii IX, 1910.

Leitner, M., *Lehrbuch des katholischen Eherechts,* Paderborn, 1902.

Lemieux, Deslisle, *The Sentence in Ecclesiastical Procedure,* Catholic University of America Canon Law Studies, n. 87, Washington, D. C.: Catholic University of America, 1934.

Leurenius, P., *Ius Canonicum Universum,* 5 vols. in 3, Venetiis, 1729.

Lijdsman, Bernardus, *Introductio in Ius Canonicum,* 2 vols., Hilvershum in Hollandia, 1924-1929.

Lydon, P. J., *Ready Answers in Canon Law,* 3. ed., New York: Benziger Brothers, 1948.

Many, S., *Praelectiones de sacra ordinatione,* Parisiis, 1905.

Maroto, Philippus, *Institutiones Iuris Canonici ad Normam Novi Codicis,* 2 vols., Vol. I, *Tractatus Fundamentales,* 3. ed., Romae: apud Commentarium pro Religiosis, 1921.

Martène, Edmundus, *De Antiquis Ecclesiae Ritibus,* 3 vols., Rotomagi, 1700-1702.

Maskell, Wm., *Monumenta Ritualia Ecclesiae Anglicanae,* 3 vols., London, 1846-1847.

McCloud, H. J., *Clerical Dress and Insignia of the Roman Catholic Church,* Milwaukee: Bruce, 1948.

McGrath, James, *The Privilege of the Canon,* Catholic University of America Canon Law Studies, n. 242, Washington, D. C.: Catholic University of America Press, 1946.

McNeill, John T., and Gamer, Helena M., *Medieval Handbooks of Penance,* Records of Civilization: Sources and Studies, Columbia University, No. XXIX, New York: Columbia University Press, 1938.

Michiels, Gommarus, *Normae Generales Iuris Canonici,* 2. ed., 2 vols., Paris: Desclée et Socii, 1949.

Migne, Jacques Paul, *Patrologiae Cursus Completus, Series Graeca,* 161 vols., Parisiis, 1857-1866.

———, *Patrologiae Cursus Completus, Series Latina,* 221 vols., Parisiis, 1844-1855.

Naz, R., *Traité de Droit Canonique,* 5 books in 4 tomes, Paris: Letouzey et Ané, 1947-1948. Tome IV, lib. 5, ed. E. Jombart, *Des Délits et des Peines.*

O'Neill, Francis J., *The Dismissal of Religious in Temporary Vows,* Catholic University of America Canon Law Studies, n. 166, Washington, D. C.: Catholic University of America Press, 1942.

Ottaviani, Alaphridus, *Institutiones Iuris Publici Ecclesiastici,* 2. ed., 2 vols., Romae: Typis Polyglottis Vaticanis, 1935-1936.

Panormitanus, Abbas (Nicolaus de Tudeschis), *Commentaria in Quinque Libros Decretalium,* 5 vols. in 7, Venetiis, 1588.

Pellé, P., *Le Droit Pénal de l'Église,* Paris: P. Lethielleux, 1939.

Prümmer, Dominicus M., *Manuale Iuris Canonici,* 4. et 5. ed., Friburgi Brisgoviae: Herder and Co., 1927.

Regatillo, E. F., *Institutiones Iuris Canonici,* 2 vols., Santander: Sal Terrae, 1941-1942.

Reiffenstuel, Anacletus, *Ius Canonicum Universum,* 5 vols. in 6, Romae, 1831-1834.

Roberti, F., *De Delictis et Poenis,* 1 vol. in 2 parts, 2. ed. revised, Romae: apud Custodiam Librariam Pontificii Instituti Utriusque Iuris, 1944.

———, *De Processibus,* Vol. I, 2. ed., Romae: apud Aedes Facultatis Iuridicae ad S. Apollinaris, 1941.

Ryan, Gerald A., *Principles of Episcopal Jurisdiction,* Catholic University of America Canon Law Studies, n. 120, Washington, D. C.: Catholic University of America Press, 1939.

Sägmüller, Johann Baptist, *Lehrbuch des katholischen Kirchenrechts,* 4. ed., Vol. I, 4 fascicles, Freiburg im Breisgau, 1925-1934.

Salucci, R., *Il Diritto Penale secondo il Codice di Diritto Canonico,* 2 vols. in 1, Subiaco: Tipografia dei Monasteri, 1926-1930.

Santi, Franciscus,-Leitner, Martinus, *Praelectiones Iuris Canonici,* 4. ed., 5 vols. in 4, Ratisbonae, 1903-1905.

Schaff, P., and Wace, H., *Nicene and Post-Nicene Fathers of the Christian Church,* Second Series, 2 vols., New York, 1890.

Schäfer, Timotheus, *Compendium de Religiosis ad Normam Codicis Iuris Canonici,* 3. ed., Romae: S. A. L. E. R., 1940.

Schmalzgrueber, Franciscus, *Ius Ecclesiasticum Universum,* 5 vols. in 12, Romae, 1843-1845.

Scott, *The Civil Law,* 17 vols. in 7, Cincinnati: The Central Trust Co., 1932.

Sipos, Stephanus, *Enchiridion Iuris Canonici,* Pécs: Ex Typographis "Haladás R. T.," 1926.

Smith, S., *Elements of Ecclesiastical Law,* 3 vols., Vol. II (*Ecclesiastical Trials*), 3. ed., New York, 1888.

Sole, J., *Praelectiones in Lib. V Codicis Iuris Canonici, De Delictis et Poenis,* Romae: Pustet, 1920.

Stephenson, Carl, *Medieval History,* New York: Harper & Bros., 1935.

Sweeney, Francis P., *The Reduction of Clerics to the Lay State,* Catholic University of America Canon Law Studies, n. 223, Washington, D. C.: Catholic University of America Press, 1945.

Van Espen, Zegerus, *Ius Ecclesiasticum Universum,* 5 vols. in 2, Coloniae Agrippinae, 1729.

Van Hove, A., *Commentarium Lovaniense in Codicem Iuris Canonici,* Mechliniae-Romae: H. Dessain; Vol. I, tom. I, *Prolegomena ad Codicem Iuris Canonici,* 1928; Vol. I, tom II, *De Legibus Ecclesiasticis,* 1930.

Vermeersch, Arturus-Creusen, Iosephus, *Epitome Iuris Canonici,* 3 vols., Vol. I, 6. ed., 1937; Vol. II, 5. ed., 1934; Vol. III, 5. ed., 1936, Mechliniae-Romae: Dessain, 1934-1937.

Wernz, Franciscus X., *Ius Decretalium,* 1. ed., 6 vols., Prati et Romae, 1898-1913.

Wernz, F.-Vidal, P., *Ius Canonicum ad Codicis Normam Exactum,* 7 toms. in 8 vols., Romae: apud Aedes Universitatis Gregorianae, 1923-1938.

Woywod, Stanislaus, *A Practical Commentary on the Code of Canon Law,* revised and enlarged edition, 2 vols., New York: Wagner, 1948.

Articles

Cappello, F., "Irrogatio Poenae per Modum Praecepti extra Iudicium," *Periodica de Re Morali, Canonica, Liturgica,* XIX (1930), 36*-38*.

Goyeneche, S., "Consultatio," *Commentarium pro Religiosis et Missionariis,* XIX (1938), 163-166.

Noval, I., "De Ratione Corrigendi et Puniendi sive in Iudicio sive extra Iure Codicis I. C.," *Jus Pontificium,* II, fasc. 4 (Oct.-Dec., 1922), 147-156.

Roberti, F., "Quaenam Poenae Applicari Possint per Modum Praecepti?" *Apollinaris,* IV (1931), 294-300.

Roelker, E., "An Introduction to the Rules of Law," Part I, *The Jurist,* X, n. 3 (July, 1950), 271-303.

Periodicals

Apollinaris, Romae, 1928-

Commentarium pro Religiosis et Missionariis (prior to 1935 *Commentarium pro Religiosis*), Romae, 1920-

Jurist, The, Washington, D. C., 1941-

Jus Pontificium, Romae, 1921-1940.

Periodica de Religiosis et Missionariis, 8 vols., Brugis, 1905-1919; from 1920: *Periodica de Re Canonica et Morali utilia praesertim Religiosis et Missionariis,* 7 vols., Brugis, 1920-1927; from 1927: *Periodica de Re Morali, Canonica, Liturgica,* Brugis (1927-1936), et Romae, 1937-

ABBREVIATIONS

AAS—*Acta Apostolicae Sedis*
Bruns—*Canones Apostolorum et Conciliorum Saeculorum IV-VII*
C—Codex Iustinianus, vel Causa
CIC—*Codex Iuris Canonici*
CSEL—*Corpus Scriptorum Ecclesiasticorum Latinorum*
C. Th.—Codex Theodosianus
D—Digesta Iustiniana
Fontes—*Codicis Iuris Canonici Fontes cura . . . Gasparri editi*
Hardouin—*Acta Conciliorum, etc.*
JE—Jaffé, *Regesta Pontificum Romanorum* (edited by Ewald; for the years 590-882)
JK—Jaffé, *op. cit.* (edited by Kaltenbrunner; to the year 590)
JL—Jaffé, *op. cit* (edited by Loewenfeld; for the years 882-1198)
Mansi—*Sacrorum Conciliorum Nova et Amplissima Collectio*
MGH—*Monumenta Germaniae Historica*
MPG—Migne, *Patrologia Graeca*
MPL—Migne, *Patrologia Latina*
N—Novellae Iustinianae
Schaff—*Nicene and Post-Nicene Fathers of the Christian Church*

ALPHABETICAL INDEX

BIOGRAPHICAL NOTE

Joseph A. Shields was born on September 27, 1923, at Philadelphia, Pennsylvania. He received his primary education at the parochial school of St. Edward the Confessor in the same city. After being graduated from Northeast Catholic High School there, he entered the Philadelphia Archdiocesan Seminary of St. Charles Borromeo on September 26, 1941. While there, he received the degree of Bachelor of Arts in June of 1947. He was ordained to the Sacred Priesthood in Philadelphia on May 26, 1949. The following October he entered the Catholic University of America to pursue graduate studies in the School of Canon Law. He received the Baccalaureate Degree in Canon Law in June, 1950, and the Licentiate Degree in Canon Law in June, 1951.

CANON LAW STUDIES*

327. KOESLER, REV. LEO J., O.S.B., J.C.D., Entrance into the Novitiate by Clerics in Major Orders (Canon 542, 2°).
328. McFARLAND, REV. NORMAN E., J.C.D., Essential Conditions and Sufficient Signs of Vocation to the Religious Life.
329. WIEST, REV. DONALD HERMAN, O.F.M. CAP., S.T.B., J.C.D., The Precensorship of Books.
330. DE WITT, REV. MAX GEORGE, A.B., J.C.D., The Cessation of Delegated Power.
331. MATHIS, REV. MARCIAN JOHN, O.F.M., J.C.D., The Constitution and Supreme Administration of Regional Seminaries Subject to the Sacred Congregation for the Propagation of the Faith in China.
332. SCHORR, REV. GEORGE F., A.B., J.C.D., The Law of the Celebret.
333. SHEEHY, REV. ROBERT FRANCIS, A.B., J.C.D., The Sacred Congregation of the Sacraments: Its Competence in the Roman Curia.
334. SHIELDS, REV. JOSEPH A., A.B., J.C.L., Deprivation of the Clerical Garb.
335. URICHECK, REV. GEORGE EDWARD, A.B., J.C.L., De forma celebrationis matrimonii in Ecclesiis Orientalibus ante Motu Proprio *Crebrae Allatae* et post.
336. DE PAUW, REV. GOMMAR A., J.C.D., The Legal Status of Catholic Elementary Schools in Belgium, 1830-1950.

*For a complete list of the available numbers of this series apply to the Catholic University of America Press, 620 Michigan Avenue, N.E., Washington 17, D. C.

www.ingramcontent.com/pod-product-compliance
Lightning Source LLC
LaVergne TN
LVHW050229080826
844660LV00012B/502

* 9 7 8 0 8 1 3 2 2 5 0 5 0 *